Ormond

ORMOND;

OR,

THE SECRET WITNESS.

By B. C. BROWN,

AUTHOR OF WIELAND, OR TRANSFORMATION.

IN THREE VOLUMES.

VOL. II.

" Sæpe intereunt aliis meditantes necem."
PHÆDRUS.

" Those who plot the destruction of others, very often fall
" themselves the victims."

PHILADELPHIA PRINTED,
LONDON, RE-PRINTED FOR HENRY COLBURN,
ENGLISH AND FOREIGN PUBLIC LIBRARY,
CONDUIT-STREET, BOND-STREET.

1811.

B. Clarke, Printer, Well-Street, London.

ORMOND,

OR THE

SECRET WITNESS

CHAP. I.

ON leaving Mr. Ormond's house, Constance was met by that gentleman. He saw her as she came out, and was charmed with the simplicity of her appearance. On entering, he interrogated the servant as to the business that brought her thither.

So, said he, as he entered the drawing-room, where Craig was seated, you have had a visitant. She came, it seems, on a pressing occasion, and would be put off with nothing but a letter.

Craig had not expected this address, but it only precipitated the execution of

a design that he had formed. Being
aware of this or similar accidents, he had
constructed and related on a previous occasion to Ormond a story suitable to his
purpose.

Aye, said he, in a tone of affected compassion, it is a sad affair enough. I am
sorry 'tis not in my power to help the
poor girl. She is wrong in imputing her
father's misfortunes to me, but I know
the source of her mistake. Would to
heaven it was in my power to repair the
wrongs they have suffered, not from me,
but from one whose relationship is a disgrace to me.

Perhaps, replied the other, you are
willing to explain this affair.

Yes, I wish to explain it. I was afraid
of some such accident as this. An explanation is due to my character. I have
already told you my story. I mentioned
to you a brother of mine. There is
scarcely thirteen months difference in our
ages. There is a strong resemblance be-

tween him and me in our exterior, though
I hope there is none at all in our minds.
This brother was a partner of a gentleman, the father of this girl, at New-
York. He was a long time nothing
better than an apprentice to Mr. Dudley,
but he advanced so much in the good
graces of his master, that he finally took
him into partnership. I did not know
till I arrived on the continent the whole
of his misconduct. It appears that he
embezzled the property of the house, and
fled away with it, and the consequence
was, that his quondam master was ruined.
I am often mistaken for my brother, to
my no small inconvenience : but all this
I told you formerly. See what a letter
I just now received from this girl.

Craig was one of the most plausible
of men. His character was a standing
proof of the vanity of physiognomy.
There were few men who could refuse
their confidence to his open and ingenuous aspect. To this circumstance,

perhaps, he owed his ruin. His temptations to deceive were stronger than what
are incident to most other men. Deception was so easy a task, that the difficulty
lay, not in infusing false opinions re pect-
ing him, but in preventing them from
being spontaneously imbibed. He contracted habits of imposture imperceptibly.
In, proportion as he deviated from the
practice of truth, he discerned the necessity of extending and systematizing his
efforts, and of augmenting the original
benignity and attractiveness of his looks,
by studied additions. The further he
proceeded, the more difficult it was to
return. Experience and habit added
daily to his speciousness, till at length
the world perhaps might have been
searched in vain for his competitor.

He had been introduced to Ormond
under the most favourable auspices. He
had provided against a danger which he
knew to be imminent, by relating his own
story as if it were his brother's. He had,

however, made various additions to it,
serving to aggravate the heinousness of
his guilt. This arose partly from policy,
and partly from the habit of lying, which
was prompted by a fertile invention, and
rendered inveterate by incessant exercise.
He interwove in his tale an intrigue between Miss Dudley and his brother.
The former was seduced, and this man
had employed his skill in chirographical
imitation, in composing letters from Miss
Dudley to his brother, which sufficiently
attested her dishonour. He and his brother, he related, to have met in Jamaica,
where the latter died, by which means
his personal property and papers came
into his possession.

Ormond read the letter which his companion presented to him on this occasion.
The papers which Craig had formerly
permitted him to inspect had made him
similiar with her hand-writing. The
penmanship was, indeed, similar, yet this

was written in a spirit not quite congenial
with that which had dictated her letters
to her lover. But he reflected that the
emergency was extraordinary, and that
the new scenes through which she had
passed, had, perhaps, enabled her to re-
trieve her virtue and enforce it. The
picture which she drew of her father's
distresses affected him and his companion
very differently. He pondered on it for
some time in silence; he then looked up,
and with his usual abruptness said, I suppose you gave her something?

No. I was extremely sorry that it
was not in my power. I have nothing
but a little trifling silver about me. I
I have no more at home than will barely
suffice to pay my board here, and my ex-
pences to Baltimore. Till I reach there
I cannot expect a supply. I was less
uneasy I confess on this account, because
I knew you to be equally willing and
much more able to afford the relief she
asks.

This Mr. Ormond had predetermined to do. He paused only to deliberate in what manner it could, with most propriety, be done. He was always willing, when he conferred benefits, to conceal the author. He was not displeased when gratitude was misplaced, and readily allowed his instruments to act as if they were principals. He questioned not the veracity of Craig, and was, therefore, desirous to free him from the molestation that was threatened in the way which had been prescribed. He put a note of one hundred dollars into his hand, and enjoined him to send it to the Dudleys that evening, or early the next morning. I am pleased, he added, with the style of this letter: It can be of no service to you ; leave it in my possession.

Craig would much rather have thrown it into the fire; but he knew the character of his companion, and was afraid to make any objection to his request. He promised to send, or carry the note the

next morning, before he set out on his
intended journey.

This journey was to Baltimore, and
was undertaken so soon merely to oblige
his friend, who was desirous of remitting
to Baltimore a considerable sum in English guineas, and who had been for some
time in search of one who might execue
this commission with fidelity. The offer
of Craig had been joyfully accepted, and
next morning had been the time fixed for
his departure, a period the most oppor-
tune for Craig's designs that could be
imagined. To return to Miss Dudley.

The sum that remained to her after
the discharge of her debts would quickly
be expended. It was no argument of
wisdom to lose sight of the future in the
oblivion of present care. The time
would inevitably come when new re-
sources would be necessary. Every hour
brought nearer the period without facili-
tating the discovery of new expedients.
She related the recent adventure to her

father. He acquiesced in the propriety
of her measures, but the succour that
she had thus obtained consoled him but
little. He saw how speedily it would
again be required, and was hopeless of a
like fortunate occurrence.

Some days had elapsed, and Constantia
had been so fortunate as to procure some
employment. She was thus engaged in
the evening when they were surprised by
a visit from their landlord. This was an
occurrence that foreboded them no good.
He entered with abruptness, and scarcely
noticed the salutations that he received.
His bosom swelled with discontent, which
seemed ready to be poured out upon his
two companions. To the inquiry as to
the condition of his health and that of his
family, he surlily answered: Never mind
how I am: none the better for my tenants I think. Never was a man so much
plagued as I have been; what with one
putting me off from time to time; what
with another quarrelling about terms,

and denying his agreement, and another
running away in my debt, I expect nothing but to come to poverty, God help
me at last : but this was the worst of all.
I was never before treated so in all my
life. I don't know what or when I shall
get to the end of my troubles. To be
fobbed out of my rent and twenty-five
dollars into the bargain ! It is very
strange treatment, I assure you, Mr.
Dudley.

What is it you mean ? replied that
gentleman. You have received your
dues, and—

Received my dues, indeed ! High
enough too ! I have received none of my
dues. I have been imposed upon. I
have been put to very great trouble, and
expect some compensation. There is no
knowing the character of one's tenants.
There is nothing but knavery in the
world one would think. I'm sure no man
has suffered more by bad tenants than I
have. But this is the strangest treat-

ment I ever met with. Very strange
indeed, Dudley, and I must be paid without delay. To lose my rent and twenty-
five dollars into the bargain, is too hard.
I never met with the equal of it, not I:
besides, I wou'dn't be put to all this
trouble for twice the sum.

What does all this mean, Mr. M'Crea?
You seem inclined to scold; but I cannot conceive why you came here for that
purpose. This behaviour is improper—

No, it is very proper, and I want payment of my money. Fifty dollars you
owe me. Miss comes to pay me my rent
as I thought. She brings me a fifty dol-
lar note; I changes it for her, for I
thought to be sure I was quite safe: but,
behold, when I sends it to the bank to get
the money, they sends me back word that
it's forged, and calls on me, before a magistrate, to tell them where I got it from.
I'm sure I never was so flustered in my
life. I would not have such a thing for
ten times the sum.

He proceeded to descant on his loss
without any interruption from his audi-
tors, whom this intelligence had struck
dumb. Mr. Dudley instantly saw the
origin and full extent of this misfortune.
He was, nevertheless, calm, and indulged
in no invectives against Craig. It is all
of a piece, said he: our ruin is inevita-
ble. Well then, let it come.

After M'Crea had railed himself
weary, he flung out of the house, warning them that next morning he should
distrain for his rent, and, at the same
time, sue them for the money that Constance had received in exchange for her
note.

Miss Dudley was unable to pursue her
task. She laid down her needle, and
fixed her eyes upon her father. They
had been engaged in earnest discourse
when their landlord entered. Now there
was a pause of profound silence, till the
affectionate Lucy, who sufficiently com-
prehended this scene, gave vent to her

affliction in sobs. Her mistress turned to her:

Cheer up, my Lucy. We shall do well enough, my girl. Our s'ate is bad enough, without doubt, but despair will make it worse.

The anxiety that occupied her mind related less to herself than to her father. He, indeed in the present instance, was exposed to prosecution. It was he who was answerable for the debt, and whose person would be thrown into durance by the suit that was menaced. The horrors of a prison had not hitherto been experienced or anticipated. The worst evil that she had imagined was inexpressibly inferior to this. The idea had in it something of terrific and loathsome. The mere supposition of its being possible was not to be endured. If all other expedients should fail, she thought of nothing less than desperate resistance. No. It was better to die than to go to prison.

For a time she was deserted of her admirable equanimity. This, no doubt, was the result of surprise. She had not yet obtained the calmness necessary to deliberation. During this gloomy interval, she would, perhaps, have adopted any scheme, however dismal and atrocious, which her father's despair might suggest. She would not refuse to terminate her own and her father's unfortunate existence by poison or the cord.

This confusion of mind could not exist long; it gradually gave place to cheerful prospects. The evil perhaps was not without its timely remedy. The person whom she had set out to visit, when her course was diverted by Craig, she once more resolved to apply to; to lay before him, without reserve, her father's situation, to entreat pecuniary succour, and to offer herself as a servant in his family, or in that of any of his friends who stood in need of one. This resolution, in a

slight degree, consoled her; but her mind
had been too thoroughly disturbed to allow her any sleep during that night.

She equipped herself betimes, and proceeded with a doubting heart to the house
of Mr. Melbourne. She was informed
that he had risen, but was never to be
seen at so early an hour. At nine o'clock
he would be disengaged, and she would
be admitted. In the present state of her
affairs this delay was peculiarly unwelcome. At breakfast, her suspense and
anxieties would not allow her to eat a
morsel; and when the hour approached
she prepared herself for a new attempt.

As she went out, she met at the door
a person whom she recognized, and whose
office she knew to be that of a constable.
Constantia had exercised, in her present
narrow sphere, that beneficence which
she had formerly exerted in a larger.
There was nothing, consistent with her
slender means, that she did not willingly
perform for the service of others. She

had not been sparing of consolation and
personal aid in many cases of personal
distress that had occurred in her neigh-
bourhood　Hence, as far as she was
known, she was reverenced.

The wife of their present visitant had
experienced her succour and sympathy,
on occasion of the death of a favourite
child. The man, notwithstanding his
office, was not of a rugged or ungrateful temper. The task that was now imposed upon him he undertook with extreme reluctance. He was somewhat reconciled to it by the reflection that another might not perform it with that gentleness and lenity which he found in himself a disposition to exercise on all occasions, but particularly on the present.

She easily guessed at his business, and
having greeted him with the utmost friend-
liness, returned with him into the house.
She endeavoured to remove the embarrassment that hung about him, but in vain.
Having levied what the law very proper-

ly calls a distress, he proceeded, after much hesitation, to inform Dudley that he was charged with a message from a magistrate, summoning him to come forthwith, and account for having a forged bank-note in his possession.

M‘Crea had given no intimation of this. The painful surprise that it produced soon yielded to a just view of this affair. Temporary inconvenience and vexation was all that could be dreaded from it. Mr. Dudley hated to be seen or known. He usually walked out in the dusk of evening, but limited his perambulations to a short space. At all other times he was obstinately recluse. He was easily persuaded by his daughter to allow her to perform this unwelcome office in his stead. He had not received, nor even seen the note. He would have willingly spared her the mortification of a judicial examination, but he knew that this was unavoidable. Should he comply with this summons himself, his daugh-

ter's presence would be equally necessary.

Influenced by these considerations, he
was willing that his daughter should ac-
company the messenger, who was content
that they should consult their mutual convenience in this respect. This interview
was to her not without its terrors; but
she cherished the hope that it might ulti-
mately conduce to good. She did not
foresee the means by which this would be
effected, but her heart was lightened by
a secret and inexplicable faith in the pro-
pitiousness of some event that was yet to
occur. This faith was powerfully en-
forced when she reached the magistrate's
door, and found that he was no other than
Melbourne, whose succour she intended
to solicit. She was speedily ushered, not
into his office, but into a private apartment, where he received her alone.

He had been favourably prepossessed
with regard to her character by the report of the officer, who, on being charged

with the message, had accounted for the
regret which he manifested, by dwelling
on the merits of Miss Dudley. He behaved with grave civility, requested her
to be seated, and accurately scrutinized
her appearance. She found herself not
deceived in her preconceptions of this
gentleman's character, and drew a favourable omen as to the event of this interview by what had already taken place.
He viewed her in silence for some time,
and then, in a conciliating tone, said :

It seems to me, madam, as if I had seen
you before. Your face, indeed, is of that
kind which, when once seen, is not easily
forgotten. I know it is a long time since,
but I cannot tell when or where. If you
will not deem me impertinent, I will venture to ask you to assist my conjectures.
Your name, as I am informed, is Acworth.——I ought to have mentioned
that Mr. Dudley, on his removal from
New-York, among other expedients to
obliterate the memory of his former con-

dition, and conceal his poverty from the world, had made this change in his name.

That, indeed, said the lady, is the name which my father at present bears. His real name is Dudley. His abode was formerly in Queen-Street, New-York. Your conjecture, Sir, is not erroneous. This is not the first time we have seen each other. I well recollect your having been at my father's house in the days of his prosperity.

Is it possible? exclaimed Mr. Melbourne, starting from his seat in the first impulse of his astonishment: are you the daughter of my friend Dudley, by whom I have so often been hospitably entertained? I have heard of his misfortunes, but knew not that he was alive, or in what part of the world he resided.

You are summoned on a very disagreeable affair, but I doubt not you will easily exculpate your father. I am told that he is blind, and that his situation is by no means as comfortable as might be

wished. I am grieved that he did not
confide in the friendship of those that
knew him. What could prompt him to
conceal himself?

My father has a proud spirit. It is
not yet broken by adversity. He disdains
to beg, but I must now assume *that office*
for his sake. I came hither this morning
to lay before you his situation, and to
entreat your assistance to save him from
a prison. He cannot pay for the poor
tenement he occupies; and our few goods
are already under distress. He has likewise contracted a debt. He is, I suppose, already sued on this account, and
must go to gaol, unless saved by the interposition of some friend.

It is true, said Melbourne, I yester-
day granted a warrant against him at the
suit of Malcolm M'Crea. Little did I
think that the defendant was Stephen
Dudley; but you may dismiss all appre-
hensions on that score. That affair shall
be settled to your father's satisfaction:

meanwhile we will, if you please, dis-
patch this unpleasant business respecting
a counterfeit note received in payment
from you by this M'Crea.

Miss Dudley satisfactorily explained
that affair. She stated the relation in
which Craig had formerly stood to her
father, and the acts of which he had been
guilty. She slightly touched on the distresses which the family had undergone
during their abode in this city, and the
means by which she had been able to pre-
serve her father from want. She mentioned the circumstances which compelled
her to seek his charity as the last re-
source, and the casual encounter with
Craig, by which she was for the present
diverted from that design. She laid before him a copy of the letter she had
written, and explained the result in the
gift of the note which now appeared to
be a counterfeit. She concluded with
stating her present views, and soliciting
him to receive her into his family, in qua-

lity of a servant, or use his interest with
some of his friends to procure a provision
of this kind. This tale was calculated
deeply to affect a man of Mr. Melbourne's humanity.

No, said he, I cannot listen to such a
request. My inclination is bounded by
my means. These will not allow me to
place you in an independent situation;
but I will do what I can. With your
leave, I will introduce you to my wife
in your true character. Her good sense
will teach her to set a just value on your
friendship. There is no disgrace in earn-
ing your subsistence by your own industry. She and her friends will furnish
you with plenty of materials; but if there
ever be a deficiency, look to me for a
supply.

Constantia's heart overflowed at this
declaration. Her silence was more elo-
quent than any words could have been.
She declined an immediate introduction
to his wife, and withdrew; but not till

her new friend had forced her to accept some money.

Place it to account, said he. It is merely paying you before hand, and discharging a debt at the time when it happens to be most useful to the creditor.

To what entire and incredible reverses is the tenor of human life subject! A short minute shall effect a transition from a state utterly destitute of hope, to a condition where all is serene and abundant. The path, which we employ all our exertions to shun, is often found, upon trial, to be the true road to prosperity.

Constantia retired from this interview with a heart bounding with exultation. She related to her father all that had happened. He was pleased on her account, but the detection of his poverty by Melbourne was the parent of new mortification. His only remaining hope relative to himself was that he should die in his obscurity, whereas, it was probable that his old acquaintance would trace him to his covert. This prognostic filled him with the deepest inquietude, and all the reasonings of his daughter were insufficient to appease him.

Melbourne made his appearance in the afternoon. He was introduced by Constantia to her father. Mr. Dudley's figure was emaciated, and his features corroded by his ceaseless melancholy. His blindness produced in them a woeful and wildering expression. His dress betokened his penury, and was in unison with the meanness of his habitation and furniture. The visitant was struck with the melancholy contrast, which these appearances exhibited, to the joyousness and splendour that he had formerly witnessed.

Mr. Dudley received the salutations of his guest with an air of embarrassment and dejection. He resigned to his daughter the task of sustaining the conversation, and excused himself from complying with the urgent invitations of

Melbourne, while at the same time he
studiously forebore all expressions tend-
ing to encourage any kind of intercourse
between them.

The guest came with a message from
his wife, who entreated Miss Dudley's
company to tea with her that evening,
adding that she should be entirely alone.
It was impossible to refuse compliance
with this request. She cheerfully as-
sented, and in the evening was introduced to Mrs. Melbourne by her husband.

Constantia found in this lady nothing
that called for reverence or admiration,
though she could not deny her some portion of esteem. The impression which
her own appearance and conversation
made upon her entertainer was much
more powerful and favourable. A consciousness of her own worth, and disdain
of the malevolence of fortune, perpetu-
ally shone forth in her behaviour. It
was modelled by a sort of mean between

presumption on the one hand, and humility on the other. She claimed no more than what was justly due to her, but she claimed no less. She did not soothe our vanity nor fascinate our pity by diffident reserves and flutterings. Neither did she disgust by arrogant negligence, and uncircumspect loquacity.

At parting she received commissions in the way of her profession, which supplied her with abundant and profitable employment. She abridged her visit on her father's account, and parted from her new friend just early enough to avoid meeting with Ormond, who entered the house a few minutes after she had left it.

What pity, said Melbourne to him, you did not come a little sooner. You pretend to be a judge of beauty. I should like to have heard your opinion of a face that has just left us.

Describe it, said the other.

That is beyond my capacity. Complexion, and hair, and eyebrows may be

painted, but these are of no great value in
the present case. It is in the putting them
together that nature has here shewn her
skill, and not in the structure of each of
the parts, individually considered. Perhaps you may at some time meet each
other here. If a lofty fellow like you,
now, would mix a little common sense
with his science, this girl might hope
for a husband, and her father for a natural protector.

Are they in search of one or the other?

I cannot say they are. Nay, I imagine
they would bear any imputation with
more patience than that, but certain I
am, they stand in need of them. How
much would it be to the honour of a
man like you rioting in wealth, to divide
it with one, lovely and accomplished as
this girl is, and struggling with indi-
gence.

Melbourne then related the adventure
of the morning. It was easy for Ormond
to perceive that this was the same person

of whom he already had some knowledge
—but there were some particulars in the
narrative that excited surprise. A note
had been received from Craig, at the first
visit in the evening, and this note was
for no more than fifty dollars. This did
not exactly tally with the information received from Craig. But this note was
forged. Might not this girl mix a little
imposture with her truth? Who knows
her temptations to hypocrisy? It might
have been a present from another quarter, and accompanied with no very ho-
nourable conditions. Exquisite wretch!
Those whom honesty will not let live
must be knaves. Such is the alternative
offered by the wisdom of society.

He listened to the tale with apparent
indifference. He speedily shifted the
conversation to new topics, and put an
end to his visit sooner than ordinary.

CHAP. II.

I know no task more arduous than a just delineation of the character of Or-mond.   To scrutinize and ascertain our own principles is abundantly difficult. To exhibit these principles to the world with absolute sincerity can hardly be expected.   We are prompted to conceal and to feign by a thousand motives; but truly to pourtray the motives, and relate the actions of another, appears utterly impossible.   The attempt, however, if made with fidelity and diligence, is not without its use.

To comprehend the whole truth with regard to the character and conduct of another, may be denied to any human being, but different observers will have, in their pictures, a greater or less portion of this truth.   No representation will be

wholly false, and some, though not perfectly, may yet be considerably exempt
from error.

Ormond was of all mankind the being
most difficult and most deserving to be
studied. A fortunate concurrence of incidents has unveiled his actions to me
with more distinctness than to any other.
My knowledge is far from being absolute, but I am conscious of a kind of
duty, first to my friend, and secondly to
mankind, to impart the knowledge I
possess.

I shall omit to mention the means by
which I became acquainted with his character, nor shall I enter, at this time,
into every part of it. His political pro-
jects are likely to possess an extensive influence on the future condition of this
western world. I do not conceive myself authorized to communicate a knowledge of his schemes, which I gained, in
some sort, surreptitiously, or at least, by
means of which he was not apprised. I

shall merely explain the maxims by which
he was accustomed to regulate his private
deportment.

No one could entertain loftier conceptions of human capacity than Ormond,
but he carefully distinguished between
men in the abstract, and men as they are.
The former were beings to be impelled,
by the breath of accident, in a right or
a wrong road, but whatever direction
they should receive, it was the property
of their nature to persist in it. Now
this impulse had been given. No single
being could rectify the error. It was
the business of the wise man to form a
just estimate of things, but not to attempt, by individual efforts, so chimerical an enterprize as that of promoting
the happiness of mankind. Their condition was out of the reach of a member
of a corrupt society to controul. A mor-
tal poison pervaded the whole system, by
means of which every thing received was
converted into bane and purulence,

Efforts designed to ameliorate the condition of an individual were sure of answering a contrary purpose. The principles of the social machine must be rectified, before men can be beneficially active. Our motives may be neutral or beneficent, but our actions tend merely to the production of evil.

The idea of total forbearance was not less delusive. Man could not be otherwise than a cause of perpetual operation and efficacy. He was part of a machine, and as such had not power to withhold his agency. Contiguousness to other parts, that is, to other men, was all that was necessary to render him a powerful concurrent. What then was the conduct incumbent on him? Whether he went forward, or stood still, whether his motives were malignant, or kind, or indifferent, the mass of evil was equally and necessarily augmented. It did not follow from these preliminaries that virtue and duty were terms without a meaning, but they require us to promote our own happiness and not the happiness of others. Not because the former end is intrinsically preferable, not because the happiness of others is unworthy of primary consideration, but because it is not to be attained. Our power in the present state of things is subjected to certain limits. A man may reasonably hope to accomplish his end when he proposes nothing but his own good : any other point is inaccessible.

He must not part with benevolent desire : this is a constituent of happiness. He sees the value of general and particular felicity; he sometimes paints it to his fancy, but if this be rarely done, it is in consequence of virtuous sensibility, which is afflicted on observing that his pictures are reversed in the real state of mankind. A wise man will relinquish the pursuit of general benefit, but not the desire of that benefit, or the perception of that in which this benefit consists, because these

are among the ingredients of virtue and
the sources of his happiness.

Principles, in the looser sense of that
term, have little influence on practice,
Ormond was, for the most part, governed, like others, by the influences of education and present circumstances. It
required a vigilant discernment to distin-
guish whether the stream of his actions
flowed from one or the other. His in-
come was large, and he managed it nearly
on the same principles as other men. He
thought himself entitled to all the splendour and ease which it would purchase,
but his taste was elaborate and correct.
He gratified his love of the beautiful, because the sensations it afforded were
pleasing, but made no sacrifices to the
love of distinction. He gave no expen-
sive entertainments for the sake of exciting the admiration of stupid gazers, or
the flattery or envy of those who shared
them. Pompous equipage and retinue
were modes of appropriating the esteem

of mankind which he held in profound
contempt. The garb of his attendants
was fashioned after the model suggested
by his imagination, and not in compliance
with the dictates of custom.

He treated with systematic negligence the etiquette that regulates the
intercourse of persons of a certain class.
He every where acted, in this respect,
as if he were alone, or among familiar
associates. The very appellations of Sir,
and Madam, and Mister, were, in his
apprehension, servile and ridiculous, and
as custom or law had annexed no penalty
to the neglect of these, he conformed to
his own opinions. It was easier for him
to reduce his notions of equality to practice than for most others. To level himself with others was an act of condescension and not of arrogance. It was requisite to descend rather than to rise; a task
the most easy, if we regard the obstacles
flowing from the prejudice of mankind,
but far most difficult if the motives of
the agent be considered.

That in which he chiefly placed his boast, was his sincerity To this he refused no sacrifice. In consequence of this, his deportment was disgusting to weak minds, by a certain air of ferocity and haughty negligence. He was without the attractions of candour, because he regarded not the happiness of others, but in subservience to his sincerity. Hence it was natural to suppose that the character of this man was easily understood. He affected to conceal nothing. No one appeared more exempt from the instigations of vanity. He set light by the good opinions of others, had no compassion for their prejudices, and hazarded assertions in their presence which he knew would be, in the highest degree, shocking to their previous notions. They might take it, he would say, as they list. Such were his conceptions, and the last thing he would give up was the use of his tongue. It was his way to give utterance to the suggestions of his under-

standing. If they were disadvantageous
to him in the opinions of others, it was
well. He did not wish to be regarded in
any light but the true one. He was
contented to be rated by the world at
his just value. If they esteemed him for
qualities which he did not possess, was
he wrong in rectifying their mistake:
but in reality, if they valued him for
that to which he had no claim, and
which he himself considered as contemp-
tible, he must naturally desire to shew
them their error, and forfeit that praise
which, in his own opinion, was a badge
of infamy.

In listening to his discourse, no one's
claim to sincerity appeared less question-
able. A somewhat different conclusion
would be suggested by a survey of his actions. In early youth he discovered in
himself a remarkable facility in imitating
the voice and gestures of others. His
memory was eminently retentive, and
these qualities would have rendered his

career, in the theatrical profession, illus-
trious, had not his condition raised him
above it. His talents were occasionally
exerted for the entertainment of convivial
parties and private circles, but he gradually withdrew from such scenes as he
advanced in age, and devoted his abilities
to higher purposes.

His aversion to duplicity had flowed
from experience of its evils. He had
frequently been made its victim; in consequence of this his temper had become
suspicious, and he was apt to impute deceit on occasions when others, of no in-
considerable sagacity, were abundantly
disposed to confidence. One transaction
had occurred in his life, in which the
consequences of being misled by false
appearances were of the utmost moment
to his honour and safety. The usual
mode of solving his doubts he deemed
insufficient, and the eagerness of his curiosity tempted him, for the first time,
to employ, for this end, his talents at

imitation. He therefore assumed a bor-
rowed character and guise, and performed his part with so much skill as fully to
accomplish his design. He whose mask
would have secured him from all other
attempts, was thus taken through an
avenue which his caution had overlooked,
and the hypocrisy of his pretensions unquestionably ascertained.

Perhaps, in a comprehensive view, the
success of this expedient was unfortunate.
It served to recommend this method of
encountering deceit, and informed him
of the extent of those powers which are
so liable to be abused. A subtlety much
inferior to Ormond's would suffice to recommend this mode of action. It was
defensible on no other principle than necessity. The treachery of mankind compelled him to resort to it. If they should
deal in a manner as upright and explicit
as himself, it would be superfluous. But
since they were in the perpetual use of
stratagems and artifices, it was allow-

able, he thought, to wield the same
arms.

It was easy to perceive, however, that
this practice was recommended to him
by other considerations. He was delighted with the power it conferred. It
enabled him to gain access, as if by su-
pernatural means, to the privacy of
others, and baffle their profoundest con-
trivances to hide themselves from his
view. It flattered him with the possession of something like omniscience. It
was besides an art, in which, as in others,
every accession of skill was a source of
new gratification. Compared with this
the performance of the actor is the sport
of children. This profession he was accustomed to treat with merciless ridicule,
and no doubt some of his contempt
arose from a secret comparison between
the theatrical species of imitation and
his own. He blended in his own person
the functions of poet and actor, and his
dramas were not fictitious but real. The

end that he proposed was not the amusement of a play-house mob. His were
scenes in which hope and fear exercised
a genuine influence, and in which was
maintained that resemblance to truth so
audaciously and grossly violated on the
stage.

It is obvious how many singular con-
junctures must have grown out of this
propensity. A mind of uncommon energy like Ormond's, which had occupied a
wide sphere of action, and which could
not fail of confederating its efforts with
those of minds like itself, must have given
birth to innumerable incidents, not unworthy to be exhibited by the most elo-
quent historian. It is not my business
to relate any of these. The fate of Miss
Dudley is intimately connected with his.
What influence he obtained over her destiny, in consequence of this dexterity,
will appear in the sequel.

It arose from these circumstances, that
no one was more impenetrable than Or-

mond, though no one's real character
seemed more easily discerned. The pro-
jects that occupied his attention were
diffused over an ample space ; and his
instruments and coadjutors were culled
from a field, whose bounds were those of
the civilized world. To the vulgar eye,
therefore, he appeared a man of specua-
tion and seclusion, and was equally in-
scrutible in his real and assumed characters. In his real, his intents were too
lofty and comprehensive, as well as too
assiduously shrouded from profane in-
spection for them to scan. In the latter,
appearances were merely calculated to
mislead and not to enlighten.

In his youth he had been guilty of the
usual excesses incident to his age and
character. These had disappeared and
yielded place to a more regular and cir-
cumspect system of action. In the choice
of his pleasures he still exposed himself
to the censure of the world. Yet there
was more of grossness and licentiousness

in the expression of his tenets, than in
the tenets themselves. So far as temperance regards the maintenance of health,
no man adhered to its precepts with more
fidelity, but he esteemed some species of
connection with the other sex as venial,
which mankind in general are vehement
in condemning.

In his intercourse with women he
deemed himself superior to the allurements of what is called love. His inferences were drawn from a consideration
of the physical propensities of a human
being. In his scale of enjoyments the
gratifications which belonged to these
were placed at the bottom. Yet he did
not entirely disdain them, and when they
could be purchased without the sacrifice
of superior advantages, they were sufficiently acceptable.

His mistake on this head was the result of his ignorance. He had not hitherto met with a female worthy of his
confidence. Their views were limited

and superficial, or their understandings
were betrayed by the tenderness of their
hearts. He found in them no intellectual
energy, no superiority to what he accounted vulgar prejudice, and no affinity
with the sentiments which he cherished
with most devotion. Their presence had
been capable of exciting no emotion
which he did not quickly discover to be
vague and sensual; and the uniformity
of his experience at length instilled into
him a belief, that the intellectual constitution of females was essentially defective.
He denied the reality of that passion
which claimed a similitude or sympathy
of minds as one of its ingredients.

CHAP. III.

He resided in New-York some time
before he took up his -abode in Philadelphia. He had some pecuniary concerns with a merchant of that place.—
He occasionally frequented his house,
finding, in the society which it afforded
him, scope for amusing speculation, and
opportunities of gaining a species of
knowledge of which at that time he
stood in need. There was one daughter
of the family, who of course constituted
a member of the domestic circle.

Helena Cleves was endowed with every
feminine and fascinating quality. Her
features were modified by the most transient sentiments, and were the seat of a
softness at all times blushful and be-
witching. All those graces of symmetry,
smoothness, and lustre, which assemble in

the imagination of the painter when he
calls from the bosom of her natal deep
the Paphian divinity, blended their per-
fections in the shape, complexion, and
hair of this lady. Her voice was naturally thrilling and melodious, and her
utterance clear and distinct. A musical
education had added to all these advantages the improvements of art, and no
one could swim in the dance with such
airy and transporting elegance.

It is obvious to inquire whether her
mental were, in any degree, on a level
with her exterior accomplishments.—
Should you listen to her talk, you would
be liable to be deceived in this respect.
Her utterance was so just, her phrases so
happy, and her language so copious and
correct, that the hearer was apt to be
impressed with an ardent veneration of
her abilities, but the truth is, she was
calculated to excite emotions more voluptuous than dignified. Her presence produced a trance of the senses rather than

an illumination of the seal. It was a
topic of wonder how she should have so
carefully separated the husk from the
kernel, and be so absolute a mistress of
the vehicle of knowledge, with so slender
means of supplying it: yet it is difficult
to judge but from comparison. To say
that Helena Cleves was silly or ignorant
would be hatefully unjust. Her understanding bore no disadvantageous comparison with that of the majority of her
sex, but when placed in competition with
that of some eminent females or of Ormond, it was exposed to the risk of
contempt.

This lady and Ormond were exposed
to mutual examination. The latter was
not unaffected by the radiance that envi-
roned this girl, but her true character
was easily discovered, and he was accustomed to regard her merely as an object
charming to the senses. His attention to
her was dictated by this principle. When
she sung or talked, it was not unworthy

of the strongest mind to be captivated
with her music and her elocution : but
these were the limits which he set to his
gratifications. That sensations of a different kind never ruffled his tranquillity
must not be supposed, but he too accurately estimated their consequences to
permit himself to indulge them.

Unhappily the lady did not exercise
equal fortitude. During a certain interval Ormond's visits were frequent, and
she insensibly contracted for him somewhat more than reverence. The tenor
of his discourse was little adapted to
cherish her hopes. In the declaration of
his opinions he was never withheld by
scruples of decorum, or a selfish regard
to his own interest. His matrimonial
tenets were harsh and repulsive. A woman of keener penetration would have
predicted from them the disappointment
of her wishes, but Helena's mind was
uninnured to the discussion of logical
points and the tracing of remote conse-

quences. His presence inspired feelings which would not permit her to bestow an impartial attention on his arguments. It is not enough to say that his reasonings failed to convince her : the combined influence of passion, and an unenlightened understanding, hindered her from fully comprehending them. All she gathered was a vague conception of something magnificent and vast in his character.

Helena was destined to experience the vicissitudes of fortune. Her father died suddenly and left her without provision. She was compelled to accept the invitations of a kinswoman, and live, in some sort, a life of dependance. She was not qualified to sustain this reverse of fortune in a graceful manner. She could not bear the diminution of her customary indulgences, and to these privations were added the inquietudes of a passion which now began to look with an aspect of hopelessness.

These events happened in the absence

of Ormond. On his return he made
himself acquainted with them. He saw
the extent of this misfortune to a woman
of Helena's character, but knew not in
what manner it might be effectually ob-
viated. He esteemed it incumbent on
him to pay her a visit in her new abode.
This token at least of respect or remembrance his duty appeared to prescribe.

This visit was unexpected by the lady.
Surprise is the enemy of concealment.
She was oppressed with a sense of her
desolate situation. She was sitting in her
own apartment in a museful posture.
Her fancy was occupied with the image
of Ormond, and her tears were flowing
at the thought of their eternal separation,
when he entered softly and unperceived
by her. A tap upon the shoulder was
the first signal of his presence. So critical an interview could not fail of unveiling the true state of the lady's heart.
Ormond's suspicions were excited, and

these suspicions speedily led to an explanation.

Ormond retired to ruminate on this discovery. I have already mentioned his sentiments respecting love. His feelings relative to Helena did not contradict his principles, yet the image which had formerly been exquisite in loveliness had now suddenly gained unspeakable attractions. This discovery had set the question in a new light. It was of sufficient importance to make him deliberate. He reasoned somewhat in the following manner.

Marriage is absurd. This flows from the general and incurable imperfection of the female character. No woman can possess that worth which would induce me to enter into this contract, and bind himself without power of revoking the decree to her society. This opinion may possibly be erroneous, but it is undoubtedly true with respect to Helena, and the uncertainty of the position in general will increase the necessity of caution in the present case. That woman may exist whom I should not fear to espouse.— This is not her. Some accident may cause our meeting. Shall I then disable myself, by an irrevocable obligation, from profiting by so auspicious an occurrence?

This girl's society was to be enjoyed in one of two ways. Should he consult his inclination there was little room for doubt. He had never met with one more highly qualified for that species of intercourse which he esteemed rational. No man more abhorred the votaries of licentiousness. Nothing was more detestable to him than a mercenary alliance. Personal fidelity and the existence of that passion, of which he had, in the present case, the good fortune to be the object, were indispensible in his scheme. The union was indebted for its value on the voluntariness with which it was formed, and the entire acquiescence of

the judgment of both parties in its rectitude. Dissimulation and artifice were
wholly foreign to the success of his
project. If the lady thought proper to
assent to his proposal, it was well. She
did so because assent was more eligible
than refusal.

She would, no doubt, prefer marriage.
She would deem it more conducive to
happiness. This was an error. This
was an opinion, his reasons for which he
was at liberty to state to her; at least it
was justifiable in refusing to subject
himself to loathsome and impracticable
obligations. Certain inconveniences attended women who set aside, on these occasions, the sanction of law, but these
were imaginary. They owed their force
to the errors of the sufferer. To anni-
hilate them, it was only necessary to reason justly, but allowing these inconveniences their full weight and an indis-
tructable existence, it was but a choice
of evils. Were they worse in this lady's

apprehension than an eternal and hopeless separation? Perhaps they were. If so, she would make her election accordingly. He did nothing but lay the conditions before her. If his scheme should obtain the concurrence of her unbiassed judgment he should rejoice. If not, her conduct should be influenced by him.— Whatever way she should decide, he would assist her in adhering to her decision, but would, meanwhile, furnish her with the materials of a right decision.

This determination was singular.— Many will regard it as incredible. No man it will be thought can put this deception on himself, and imagine that there was genuine beneficence in a scheme like this. Would the lady more consult her happiness by adopting than by rejecting it? There can be but one answer. It cannot be supposed that Ormond, in stating this proposal, acted with all the impartiality that he pretended; that he did not employ fallacious exaggerations and ambiguous expedients; that he did not seize every opportunity of triumphing over her weakness, and building his success rather on the illusions of her heart than the convictions of her understanding. His conclusions were specious but delusive, and were not uninfluenced by improper biases; but of this he himself was scarcely conscious, and it must be, at least, admitted that he acted with scrupulous sincerity.

An uncommon degree of skill was required to introduce this topic so as to avoid the imputation of an insult. This scheme was little in unison with all her preconceived notions. No doubt the irksomeness of her present situation, the allurements of luxury and ease which Ormond had to bestow, and the revival of her ancient independence and security, had some share in dictating her assent.

Her concurrence was by no means cordial and unhesitating. Remorse and the sense of dishonour pursued her to her retreat, though chosen with a view of shunning their intrusions, and it was only when the reasonings and blandishments of her lover were exhibited, that she was lulled into temporary tranquillity.

She removed to Philadelphia. Here she enjoyed all the consolations of opulence. She was mistress of a small but elegant mansion. She possessed all the means of solitary amusement, and frequently enjoyed the company of Ormond. These however were insufficient to render her happy. Certain reflections might, for a time, be repressed or divested of their sting, but they insinuated themselves at every interval, and imparted to her mind a hue of dejection from which she could not entirely relieve herself.

She endeavoured to acquire a relish for the pursuits of literature, by which her lonely hours might be cheered ; but of this, even in the blithsomeness and serenity of her former days, she was inca-

pable; much more so now when she
was the prey of perpetual inquietude.—
Ormond perceived this change, not without uneasiness. All his efforts to reconcile her to her present situation were
fruitless. They produced a momentary
effect upon her. The softness of her
temper and her attachment to him would,
at his bidding, restore her to vivacity and
ease, but the illumination seldom endured
longer than his presence, and the novelty
of some amusement with which he had
furnished her.

At his next visit perhaps he would
find that a new task awaited him. She
indulged herself in no recriminations or
invectives. She could not complain that
her lover had deceived her. She had
voluntarily and deliberately accepted the
conditions prescribed. She regarded her
own disposition to repine as a species of
injustice. She laid no claim to an increase of tenderness. She hinted not a
wish for a change of situation; yet she

was unhappy. Tears stole into her eyes, and her thoughts wandered into gloomy reverie, at moments when least aware of their reproach, and least willing to indulge them.

Was a change to be desired? Yes; provided that change was equally agreeable to Ormond, and should be seriously proposed by him: of this she had no hope. As long as his accents rung in her ears, she even doubted whether it were to be wished. At any rate, it was impossible to gain his approbation to it. Her destiny was fixed. It was better than the cessation of all intercourse, yet her heart was a stranger to all permanent tranquillity.

Her manners were artless and ingenuous. In company with Ormond her heart was perfectly unveiled. He was her divinity, to whom every sentiment was visible, and to whom she spontaneously uttered what she thought, because the employment was pleasing; because he listened with apparent satisfaction ; and because, in fine, it was the same thing to speak and to think in his presence. There was no inducement to conceal from him the most evanescent and fugitive ide s.

Ormond was not an inattentive or indifferent spectator of those appearances. His friend was unhappy. She shrunk aghast from her own reproaches and the censure of the world. This morbid sensibility he had endeavoured to cure, but hitherto in vain. What was the amount of her unhappiness? Her spirits had formerly been gay, but her gaiety was capable of yielding place to soul-ravishing and solemn tenderness. Her sedateness was, at those times, the offspring not of reflection but of passion. There still remained much of her former self. He was seldom permitted to witness more than the traces of sorrow. In answer to his inquiries, she, for the most part, described sensations that were gone, and which she flattered herself and him would never return ; but this hope was always doomed to disappointment. Solitude infallibly conjured up the ghost which had been laid, and it was plain that argument was no adequate remedy for this disease.

How far would time alleviate its evils? When the novelty of her condition should disappear, would she not regard it with other eyes ? By being familiar with contempt, it will lose its sting ; but is that to be wished ? Must not the character be thoroughly depraved before the scorn of our neighbours shall become indifferent? Indifference, flowing from a sense of justice, and a persuasion that our treatment is unmerited, is characteristic of the noblest minds, but indifference to obloquy because we are habituated to it is a token of peculiar baseness. This therefore was a remedy to be ardently deprecated.

He had egregiously over-rated the in-

fluence of truth and his own influence.
He had hoped that his victory was permanent. In order to the success of truth,
he was apt to imagine that nothing was
needful but opportunities for a compleat
exhibition of it. They that inquire and
reason with sufficient deliberateness and
caution must inevitably accomplish their
end. These maxims were confuted in the
present case. He had formed no advantageous conceptions of Helena's capacity.
His aversion to matrimony arose from
those conceptions, but experience had
shewn him that his conclusions, unfavourable as they were, had fallen short
of the truth. Convictions, which he had
conceived her mind to be sufficiently
strong to receive and retain, were proved
to have made no other than a momentary
impression. Hence his objections to ally
himself to a mind inferior to his own were
strengthened rather than diminished. But
he could not endure the thought of being
instrumental to her misery.

Marriage was an efficacious remedy, but he could not as yet bring himself to regard the aptitude of this cure as a subject of doubt. The idea of separation sometimes occurred to him. He was not unapprehensive of the influence of time and absence, in curing the most vehement passion, but to this expedient the lady could not be reconciled. He knew her too well to believe that she would willingly adopt it. But the only obstacle to this scheme did not flow from the lady's opposition. He would probably have found upon experiment as strong an aversion to adopt it in himself as in her.

It was easy to see the motives by which he would be likely to be swayed into a change of principles. If marriage were the only remedy, the frequent repetition of this truth must bring him insensibly to doubt the rectitude of his determinations against it. He deeply reflected on the consequences which marriage involves. He scrutinized with the utmost accuracy the character of his friend, and surveyed it in all its parts. Inclination could not fail of having some influence on his opinions. The charms of this favourite object tended to impair the clearness of his view, and extenuate or conceal her defects. He entered on the enumeration of her errors with reluctance. Her happiness, had it been wholly disconnected with his own, might have had less weight in the balance, but now, every time the scales were suspended, this consideration acquired new weight.

Most men are influenced in the formation of this contract, by regards purely physical. They are incapable of higher views. They regard with indifference every tie that binds them to their contemporaries, or to posterity. Mind has no part in the motives that guide them. They chuse a wife as they chuse any household moveable, and when the irritation of the senses has subsided, the

attachment that remains is the offspring
of habit.

Such were not Ormond's modes of
thinking. His creed was of too extraordinary a kind not to merit explication.
The terms of this contract were, in his
eyes, iniquitous and absurd. He could
not think with patience of a promise
which no time could annul, which pretended to ascertain contingencies and regulate the future. To forego the liberty
of chusing his companion, and bind himself to associate with one whom he despised; to raise to his own level whom
nature had irretrievably degraded; to
avow and persist in his adherence to a
falsehood, palpable and loathsome to his
understanding; to affirm that he was
blind, when in full possession of his
senses; to shut his eyes and grope in the
dark, and call upon the compassion of
mankind on his infirmity, when his organs were in no degree impaired, and
the scene around him was luminous and

beautiful, was an height of infatuation that he could never attain. And why should he be thus self-degraded ? Why should he take a laborious circuit to reach a point which, when attained, was trivial, and to which reason had pointed out a road short and direct ?

A wife is generally nothing more than a household superintendant. This function could not be more wisely vested than it was at present. Every thing, in his domestic system, was fashioned on strict and inflexible principles. He wanted instruments and not partakers of his authority. One whose mind was equal and not superior to the cogent apprehension and punctual performance of his will. One whose character was squared, with mathematical exactness, to his situation. Helena, with all her faults, did not merit to be regarded in this light. Her introduction would destroy the harmony of his scheme, and be, with respect to herself, a genuine de-

basement. A genuine evil would thus
be substituted for one that was purely
imaginary.

Helena's intellectual deficiencies could
not be concealed. She was a proficient
in the elements of no science. The doc-
trine of lines and surfaces was as dis-
proportionate with her intellects as with
those of the mock-bird. She had not
reasoned on the principles of human
action, nor examined the structure of
society. She was ignorant of the past or
present condition of mankind. History
had not informed her of the one, nor the
narratives of voyagers, nor the deductions
of geography of the other. The heights
of eloquence and poetry were shut out
from her view. She could not commune
in their native dialect with the sages of
Rome and Athens. To her those peren-
nial fountains of wisdom and refinement
were sealed. The constitution of nature,
the attributes of its author, the arrangement of the parts of the external uni-

verse, and the substance, modes of operation, and ultimate destiny of human
intelligence, were enigmas unsolved and
insoluble by her.

But this was not all. The super-
structure could for the present be spared.
Nay it was desirable that the province of
rearing it should be reserved for him.
All he wanted was a suitable foundation;
but this Helena did not possess. ~ He had
not hitherto been able to create in her the
inclination or the power. She had listened to his precepts with docility. She
had diligently conned the lessons which
he had prescribed, but the impressions
were as fleeting as if they had been made
on water. Nature seemed to have set
impassable limits to her attainments.

This indeed was an unwelcome belief.
He struggled to invalidate it. He re-
flected on the immaturity of her age.
What but crude and hasty views was it
reasonable to expect at so early a period.
If her mind had not been awakened, it

had proceeded, perhaps, from the injudiciousness of his plans, or merely from their not having been persisted in. What was wanting but the ornaments of mind to render this being all that poets have feigned of angelic nature. When he indulged himself in imaging the union of capacious understanding with her personal loveliness, his conceptions swelled to a pitch of enthusiasm, and it seemed as if no labour was too great to be employed in the production of such a creature. And yet, in the midst of his glowings, he would sink into sudden dejection at the recollection of that which passion had, for a time, excluded. To make her wise it would be requisite to change her sex. He had forgotten that his pupil was a female, and her capacity therefore limited by nature. This mortifying thought was outbalanced by another. Her attainments, indeed, were suitable to the imbecility of her sex; but did she not surpass, in those attainments,

the ordinary rate of women? They must
not be condemned, because they are out-
shone by qualities that are necessarily
male births.

Her accomplishments formed a much
more attractive theme. He overlooked
no article in the catalogue. He was
confounded at one time, and encouraged
at another, on remarking the contradic-
tions that seemed to be included in her
character. It was difficult to conceive
the impossibility of passing that barrier
which yet she was able to touch. She
was no poet. She listened to the re-
hearsal without emotion, or was moved,
not by the substance of the passage, by
the dazzling image, or the magic sympathy, but by something adscititious:
yet, usher her upon the stage, and no
poet could wish for a more powerful or-
gan of his conceptions. In assuming this
office, she appeared to have drank in the
very soul of the dramatist. What was
wanting in judgment was supplied by

memory, in the tenaciousness of which she has seldom been rivalled.

Her sentiments were trite and undigested, but were decorated with all the fluences and melodies of elocution. Her musical instructor had been a Sicilian, who had formed her style after the Italian model. This man had likewise taught her his own language. He had supplied her chiefly with Sicilian compositions, both in poetry and melody, and was content to be unclassical, for the sake of the feminine and voluptuous graces of his native dialect.

Ormond was an accurate judge of the proficiency of Helena, and of the felicity with which these accomplishments were suited to her character. When his pupil personated the victims of anger and grief, and poured forth the fiery indignation of Calista, or the maternal despair of Constance, or the self-contensions of Ipsipile, he could not deny the homage which her talents might claim.

Her Sicilian tutor had found her no less tractable as a votary of painting. She needed only the education of Angelica to exercise as potent and prolific a pencil. This was incompatible with her condition, which limited her attainments to the elements of this art. It was otherwise with music. Here there was no obstacle to skill, and here the assiduities of many years, in addition to a prompt and ardent genius, set her beyond the hopes of rivalship.

Ormond had often amused his fancy with calling up images of excellence in this art. He saw no bounds to the influence of habit, in augmenting the speed and multiplying the divisions of muscular motion. The fingers, by their form and size, were qualified to outrun and elude the most vigilant eye. The sensibility of keys and wires had limits, but these limits depended on the structure of the instrument, and the perfection of its tructure was proportioned to the skill of

the artist. On well constructed keys and
strings, was it possible to carry diversi-
ties of movement and pressure too far.
How far they could be carried was mere
theme of conjecture, until it was his fate
to listen to the magical performances of
Helena, whose votant finger seemed to be
self-impelled. Her touches were crea-
tive of a thousand forms of *piano*, and of
numberless transitions from grave to
quick, perceptible only to ears like her
own.

In the selection and arrangement of
notes there are no limits to luxuriance
and celerity. Helena had long relinquished the drudgery of imitation. She
never played but when there were motives to fervour, and when she was likely
to ascend without impediment, and to
maintain for a suitable period her eleva-
tion, to the element of new ideas. The
lyrics of Milton and of Metastasio she
sung with accompaniments that never
tired, because they were never repeated.

Her harp and clavichord supplied her
with endless combinations, and these in
the opinion of Ormond were not inferior
to the happiest exertions of Handel and
Arne.

Chess was his favourite amusement.
This was the only game which he allowed himself to play. He had studied it
with so much zeal and success, that
there were few with whom he deigned to
contend. He was prone to consider it as
a sort of criterion of human capacity.
He who had acquired skill in this *science*
could not be infirm in mind; and yet he
found in Helena a competitor not unworthy of all his energies. Many hours
were consumed in this employment, and
here the lady was sedate, considerate,
extensive in foresight, and fertile in expedients.

Her deportment was graceful, inasmuch as it flowed from a consciousness
of her defects. She was devoid of arrogance and vanity, neither imagining her-

self better than she was, and setting light by those qualifications which she unquestionably possessed. Such was the mixed character of this woman.

Ormond was occupied with schemes of a rugged and arduous nature. His intimate associates and the partakers of his confidence were imbued with the same zeal, and ardent in the same pursuits. Helena could lay no claim to be exalted to this rank. That one destitute of this claim should enjoy the privileges of his wife was still a supposition truly monstrous: yet the image of Helena, fondly loving him, and a model as he conceived of tenderness and constancy, devoured by secret remorse, and pursued by the scorn of mankind, a mark for slander to shoot at, and an outcast of society, did not visit his meditations in vain. The rigour of his principles began now to relent.

He considered that various occupations are incident to every man. He cannot be invariably employed in the promotion

of one purpose. He must occasionally
unbend, if he desires that the springs of
his mind should retain their full vigour.
Suppose his life were divided between
business and amusement. This was a
necessary distribution, and sufficiently
congenial with his temper. It became
him to select with skill his sources of
amusement. It is true that Helena was
unable to participate in his graver occupations; What then? In whom were
blended so many pleasurable attributes?
In her were assembled an exquisite and
delicious variety. As it was, he was
daily in her company. He should scarcely be more so if marriage should take
place. In that case, no change in their
mode of life would be necessary. There
was no need of dwelling under the same
roof. His revenue was equal to the support of many household establishments.
His personal independence would remain
equally inviolate. No time, he thought,
would diminish his influence over the

mind of Helena, and it was not to be forgotten that the transition would to her be happy. It would reinstate her in the esteem of the world, and dispel those phantoms of remorse and shame by which she was at present persecuted.

These were plausible considerations. They tended at least to shake his resolutions. Time would probably have compleated the conquest of his pride, had not a new incident set the question in a new light.

CHAP. IV.

THE narrative of Melbourne made a deeper impression on the mind of his guest than was at first apparent. This man's conduct was directed by the present impulse, and however elaborate his abstract notions, he seldom stopped to settle the agreement between his principles and actions. The use of money was a science like every other branch of benevolence, not reducible to any fixed principles. No man, in the disbursement of money, could say whether he was conferring a benefit or injury. The visible and immediate effects might be good, but evil was its ultimate and general tendency. To be governed by a view to the present rather than the future was a human infirmity from which he did not pretend to be exempt. This, though an insufficient apology for the conduct of a rational being, was suitable to his indolence, and he was content in all cases to employ it. It was thus that he reconciled himself to beneficent acts, and humourously held himself up as an object of censure, on occasions when most entitled to applause.

He easily procured information as to the character and situation of the Dudleys. Neighbours are always inquisitive, and happily, in this case, were enabled to make no unfavourable report. He resolved without hesitation to supply their wants. This he performed in a manner truly characteristic. There was a method of gaining access to families, and marking them in their unguarded attitudes more easy and effectual than any other: it required least preparation and cost least pains: the disguise also was of the most impenetrable kind. He had served a sort of occasional apprenticeship to the art, and executed its functions with perfect ease. It was the most

entire and grotesque metamorphosis ima-
ginable. It was stepping from the highest to the lowest rank in society, and
shifting himself into a form as remote
from his own as those recorded by Ovid.
In a word, it was sometimes his practice
to exchange his complexion and habili-
ments for those of a negro and a chimney-
sweep, and to call at certain doors for
employment. This he generally secured
by importunities, and the cheapness of
his services.

When the loftiness of his port, and
the punctiliousness of his nicety were
considered, we should never have believed, what yet could be truly asserted,
that he had frequently swept his own
chimneys, without the knowledge of his
own servants.* It was likewise true,
though equally incredible, that he had
played at romps with his scullion, and

* Similar exploits are related of Count de la
Lippe and Wortley Montague.

listened with patience to a thousand slanders on his own character.

In this disguise he visited the house of Mr. Dudley. It was nine o'clock in the morning. He remarked with critical eyes the minutest circumstance in the appearance and demeanour of his customers, and glanced curiously at the house and furniture. Every thing was new and every thing pleased. The walls, though broken into roughness by carelessness or time, were adorned with glistening white. The floor, though loose and uneven, and with gaping seams, had received all the improvments which cloth and brush could give. The pine tables, rush chairs, and uncurtained bed, had been purchased at half price, at vendue, and exhibited various tokens of decay, but care and neatness and order were displayed in their condition and arrangement.

The lower apartment was the eating and sitting room. It was likewise Mr.

Dudley's bed-chamber. The upper
room was occupied by Constance and her
Lucy. Ormond viewed every thing with
the accuracy of an artist, and carried
away with him a catalogue of every
thing visible. The faded form of Mr.
Dudley, that still retained its dignity,
the sedateness, graceful condescension,
and personal elegance of Constantia, were
new to the apprehension of Ormond.
The contrast between the house and its
inhabitants rendered the appearance
more striking. When he had finished
his task he retired, but returning in a
quarter of an hour, he presented a letter
to the young lady. He behaved as if by
no means desirous of eluding her inter-
rogatories, and when she desired him to
stay, readily complied. The letter, un-
signed, and without superscription, was
to this effect.

"The writer of this is acquainted with
the transaction between Thomas Craig
and Mr. Dudley. The former is debtor

to Mr. Dudley in a large sum. I have undertaken to pay as much of this debt, and at such times, as suits my convenience. I have had pecuniary engagements with Craig. I hold myself in the sum inclosed, discharging so much of his debt. The future payments are uncertain, but I hope they will contribute to relieve the necessities of Mr. Dudley."

Ormond had calculated the amount of what would be necessary for the annual subsistence of this family on the present frugal plan. He had regulated his disbursements accordingly.

It was natural to feel curiosity as to the writer of this epistle. The bearer displayed a prompt and talkative disposition. He had a staring eye and a grin of vivacity forever at command. When questioned by Constantia, he answered that the gentleman had forbidden him to mention his name or the place where he lived. Had he ever met with the same person before? O yes. He had lived

with him from a child. His mother
lived with him still and his brothers.
His master had nothing for him to do
at home, so he sent him out sweeping
chimneys, taking from him only half the
money that he earned that way. He was
a very good master.

Then the gentleman had been a long
time in the city?

O yes. All his life he reckoned. He
used to live in Walnut Street, but now
he's moved down town. Here he check-
ed himself, and added, but I forgets. I
must not tell where he lives. He told me
I must'nt.

He has a family and children, I suppose?

O yes. Why don't you know Miss
Hetty and Miss Betsy—— there again.
I was going to tell the name that he
said I must not tell.

Constantia saw that the secret might
be easily discovered, but she forbore.
She disdained to take advantage of this

messenger's imagined simplicity. She dismissed him with some small addition to his demand, and with a promise always to employ him in this way.

By this mode Ormond had effectually concealed himself. The lady's conjectures, founded on this delusive information, necessarily wandered widely from the truth. The observations that he had made during this visit afforded his mind considerable employment. The manner in which this lady had sustained so cruel a reverse of fortune, the cheerfulness with which she appeared to forego all the gratifications of affluence, the skill with which she selected her path of humble industry, and the steadiness with which she pursued it, were proofs of a moral constitution, from which he supposed the female sex to be debarred. The comparison was obvious between Constantia and Helena, and the result was by no means advantageous to the latter. Was it possible that such an one

descended to the level of her father's apprentice? That she sacrificed her honour
to a wretch like that? This reflection
tended to repress the inclination he would
otherwise have felt for cultivating her
society, but it did not indispose him to
benefit her in a certain way.

On his next visit to his "Bella Sici-
liana," as he called her, he questioned
her as to the need in which she might
stand of the services of a seamstress, and
being informed that they were sometimes
wanted, he recommended Miss Acworth
to her patronage. He said that he had
heard her spoken of in favourable terms
by the gossips at Melbourne's. They
represented her as a good girl, slenderly
provided for, and he wished that Helena
would prefer her to all others.

His recommendation was sufficient.
The wishes of Ormond, as soon as they
became known, became her's. Her temper made her always diligent in search of
novelty. It was easy to make work for

the needle. In short she resolved to send for her the next day. The interview accordingly took place on the ensuing morning, not without mutual surprise, and on the part of the fair Sicilian not without considerable embarrassment.

This circumstance arose from each having changed their respective names, though from motives of a very different kind. They were not strangers to each other, though no intimacy had ever subsisted between them. Each was merely acquainted with the name, person, and general character of the other. No circumstance in Constantia's situation tended to embarrass her. Her mind had attained a state of serene composure, incapable of being ruffled by an incident of this kind. She merely derived pleasure from the sight of her old acquaintance. The aspect of things around her was splendid and gay. She seemed the mistress of the mansion, and her name was changed.

Hence it was unavoidable to conclude that she was married.

Helena was conscious that appearances were calculated to suggest this conclusion. The idea was a painful one. She sorrowed to think that this conclusion was fallacious. The consciousness that her true condition was unknown to her visitant, and the ignominiousness of that truth, gave an air of constraint to her behaviour, which Constance ascribed to a principle of delicacy.

In the midst of reflections relative to herself, she admitted some share of surprise at the discovery of Constance in a situation so inferior to that in which she had formerly known her. She had heard in general terms of the misfortunes of Mr Dudley, but was unacquainted with particulars; but this surprise, and the difficulty of adapting her behaviour to circumstances, was only in part the source of her embarrassment, though

by her companion it was wholly attribut-
ed to this cause. Constance thought it
her duty to remove it by open and unaffected manners. She therefore said, in
a sedate and cheerful tone, You see me,
Madam, in a situation somewhat unlike
that in which I formerly was placed.
You will probably regard the change as
an unhappy one, but I assure you I have
found it far less so than I expected. I
am thus reduced not by my own fault.
It is this reflection that enables me to
conform to it without a murmur. I shall
rejoice to know that Mrs. Eden is as
happy as I am.

Helena was pleased with this address,
and returned an answer full of sweetness.
She had not in her compassion for the
fallen a particle of pride. She thought
of nothing but the contrast between the
former situation of her visitant and the
present. The fame of her great qualities
had formerly excited veneration, and that
reverence was by no means diminished by

a nearer scrutiny. The consciousness of
her own frailty meanwhile diffused over
the behaviour of Helena a timidity and
dubiousness uncommonly fascinating.
She solicited Constantia's friendship in a
manner that shewed she was afraid of
nothing but denial. An assent was eagerly given, and thenceforth a cordial intercourse was established between them.

The real situation of Helena was easily
discovered. The officious person who
communicated this information, at the
same time cautioned Constance against
associating with one of tainted reputation. This information threw some light
upon appearances. It accounted for
that melancholy which Helena was unable to conceal. It explained that solitude in which she lived, and which Constantia had ascribed to the death or absence of her husband. It justified the
solicitous silence she had hitherto maintained respecting her own affairs, and
which her friend's good sense forbad her
to employ any sinister means of eluding.

No long time was necessary to make her mistress of Helena's character. She loved her with uncommon warmth, though by no means blind to her defects. She formed no expectations from the knowledge of her character, to which this intelligence operated as a disappointment. It merely excited her pity, and made her thoughtful how she might assist her in repairing this deplorable error.

This design was of no ordinary magnitude. She saw that it was previously necessary to obtain the confidence of Helena. This was a task of easy performance. She knew the purity of her own motives and the extent of her powers, and embarked in this undertaking with full confidence of success. She had only to profit by a private interview, to acquaint her friend with what she knew, to solicit a compleat and satisfactory disclosure, to explain the impressions which her intelligence produced, and to offer her disinterested advice. No one knew better

how to couch her ideas in words suitable
to the end proposed by her in imparting
them.

Helena was at first terrified, but the
benevolence of her friend quickly entitled
her to confidence and gratitude that
knew no limits. She had been deterred
from unveiling her heart by the fear of
exciting contempt or abhorrence : but
when she found that all due allowances
were made, that her conduct was treated
as erroneous in no atrocious or inexpiable
degree, and as far from being insuscep-
tible of remedy ; that the obloquy with
which she had been treated found no
vindicator or participator in her friend,
her heart was considerably relieved. She
had been long a stranger to the sympathy
and intercourse of her own sex. Now
this good, in its most precious form, was
conferred upon her, and she experienced
an increase rather than diminution of
tenderness, in consequence of her true
situation being known.

She made no secret of any part of her history. She did full justice to the integrity of her lover, and explained the unforced conditions on which she had consented to live with him. This relation exhibited the character of Ormond in a very uncommon light. His asperities wounded, and his sternness chilled. What unauthorised conceptions of matrimonial and political equality did he entertain! He had fashioned his treatment of Helena on sullen and ferocious principles. Yet he was able, it seemed, to mould her, by means of them, nearly into the creature that he wished. She knew too little of the man justly to estimate his character. It remained to be ascertained whether his purposes were consistent and upright, or were those of a villain and betrayer.

Meanwhile what was to be done by Helena? Marriage had been refused on plausible pretences. Her unenlightened understanding made her no match for her lover. She would never maintain her claim to nuptial privileges in his presence, or if she did, she would never convince him of their validity.

Were they indeed valid? Was not the disparity between them incurable? A marriage of minds so dissimilar could only be productive of misery immediately to him, and by a reflex operation to herself. She could not be happy in a union that was the source of regret to her husband. Marriage therefore was not possible, or if possible, was not perhaps to be wished. But what was the choice that remained?

To continue in her present situation was not to be endured. Disgrace was a dæmon that would blast every hope of happiness. She was excluded from all society but that of the depraved. Her situation was eminently critical. It depended, perhaps, on the resolution she should now form whether she would be enrolled among the worst of mankind.

Infamy is the worst of evils. It creates innumerable obstructions in the paths of virtue. It manacles the hand, and entangles the feet that are active only to good. To the weak it is an evil of much greater magnitude. It determines their destiny, and they hasten to merit that reproach, which, at first it may be, they did not deserve.

This connection is intrinsically flagitious. Helena is subjected by it to the worst ills that are incident to humanity, the general contempt of mankind, and the reproaches of her own conscience. From these there is but one method from which she can hope to be relieved. The intercourse must cease.

It was easier to see the propriety of separation, than to project means for accomplishing it. It was true that Helena loved ; but what quarter was due to this passion when divorced from integrity ? Is it not in every bosom a perishable sentiment ? Whatever be her warmth, absence will congeal it. Place her in new scenes, and supply her with new associates. Her accomplishments will not fail to attract votaries. From these she may select a conjugal companion suitable to her mediocrity of talents.

But alas! what power on earth can prevail on her to renounce Ormond? Others may justly entertain this prospect, but it must be invisible to her. Besides, is it absolutely certain that either her peace of mind or her reputation will be restored by this means? In the opinion of the world her offences cannot, by any perseverance in penitence, be expiated. She will never believe that separation will exterminate her passion. Certain it is, that it will avail nothing to the re-establishment of her fame: but if it were conducive to these ends, how chimerical to suppose that she will ever voluntarily adopt it? If Ormond refuse his concurrence, there is absolutely an end to hope. And what power on earth is able to sway

. his determinations ? At least what influence was it possible for her to obtain over
them ?

Should they separate, whither should
she retire ? What mode of subsistence
should she adopt ? She has never been
accustomed to think beyond the day. She
has eaten and drank, but another has provided the means. She scarcely compre-
hends the principle that governs the
world, and in consequence of which nothing can be gained but by giving something in exchange for it. She is ignorant
and helpless as a child, on every topic that
relates to the procuring of subsistence.
Her education has disabled her from
standing alone.

But this was not all. She must not
only be supplied by others, but sustained
in the enjoyment of a luxurious existence.
Would you bereave her of the gratifications of opulence ? You had better
take away her life. Nay, it would ulti-

mately amount to this. She can live but
in one way.

At present she is lovely, and, to a certain degree, innocent, but expose her to
the urgencies and temptations of want,
let personal pollution be the price set
upon the voluptuous affluence of her
present condition, and it is to be feared
there is nothing in the contexture of her
mind to hinder her from making the purchase. In every respect therefore the
prospect was an hopeless one; so hopeless, that her mind insensibly returned to
the question which she had at first dismissed with very slight examination, the
question relative to the advantages and
probabilities of marriage. A more accurate review convinced her that this was
the most eligible alternative. It was,
likewise, most easily effected. The lady,
of course, would be its fervent advocate.
There did not want reasons why Ormond
should finally embrace it. In what

manner appeals to his reason or his passion might most effectually be made she knew not.

Helena was not qualified to be her own advocate. Her unhappiness could not but be visible to Ormond. He had shewn himself attentive and affectionate. Was it impossible that, in time, he should reason himself into a spontaneous adoption of this scheme? This, indeed, was a slender foundation for hope, but there was no other on which she could build.

Such were the meditations of Constantia on this topic. She was deeply solicitous for the happiness of her friend. They spent much of their time together. The consolations of her society were earnestly sought by Helena, but to enjoy them, she was for the most part obliged to visit the former at her own dwelling. For this arrangement, Constance apologized by saying, You will pardon my requesting you to favour me with your visits, ra-

ther than allowing you mine. Every
thing is airy and brilliant within these
walls. There is, besides, an air of seclusion and security about you that is
delightful. In comparison, my dwelling
is bleak, comfortless, and unretired, but
my father is entitled to all my care. His
infirmity prevents him from amusing
himself, and his heart is cheered by the
mere sound of my voice, though not addressed to him. The mere belief of my
presence seems to operate as an antidote
to the dreariness of solitude ; and now
you know my motives, I am sure you
will not only forgive but approve of my
request.

CHAP. V.

WHEN once the subject had been introduced, Helena was prone to descant upon her own situation, and listened with deference to the remarks and admonitions of her companion. Constantia did not conceal from her any of her sentiments. She enabled her to view her own condition in its true light, and set before her the indispensible advantages of marriage, while she, at the same time, afforded her the best directions as to the conduct she ought to pursue in order to effect her purpose.

The mind of Helena was thus kept in a state of perpetual and uneasy fluctuation. While absent from Ormond, or listening to her friend's remonstrances, the deplorableness of her condition arose in its most disastrous hues before her imagination. But the spectre seldom failed to vanish at the approach of Ormond. His voice dissipated every inquietude.

She was not insensible of this inconstancy. She perceived and lamented her own weakness. She was destitute of all confidence in her own exertions. She could not be in the perpetual enjoyment of his company. Her intervals of tranquillity therefore were short, while those of anxiety and dejection were insupportably tedious. She revered, but believed herself incapable to emulate the magnanimity of her monitor. The consciousness of inferiority, especially in a case like this, in which her happiness so much depended on her own exertions, excited in her the most humiliating sensations.

While indulging in fruitless melancholy, the thought one day occurred to her, why may not Constantia be prevailed upon to plead my cause? Her capacity and courage are equal to any undertak-

ing. The reasonings that are so powerful in my eyes, would they be trivial and
futile in those of Ormond? I cannot
have a more pathetic and disinterested
advocate.

This idea was cherished with uncommon ardour. She seized the first opportunity that offered itself to impart it to
her friend. It was a wild and singular
proposal, and was rejected at the first
glance. This scheme, so romantic and
impracticable as it at first seemed, appeared to Helena in the most plausible
colours. She could not bear to relinquish her new-born hopes. She saw no
valid objection to it. Every thing was
easy to her friend, provided her sense of
duty and her zeal could be awakened.
The subject was frequently suggested to
Constantia's reflections. Perceiving the
sanguineness of her friend's confidence,
and fully impressed with the value of the
end to be accomplished, she insensibly
veered to the same opinion; at least the

scheme was worthy of a candid discussion before it was rejected.

Ormond was a stranger to her.	His
manners were repulsive and austere.	She
was a mere girl.	Her personal attach-
ment to Helena was all that she could
plead in excuse for taking part in her
concerns.	The subject was delicate.	A
blunt and irregular character like Ormond's might throw an air of ridicule
over the scene.	She shrunk from the en-
counter of a boisterous and manlike
spirit.

But were not these scruples effeminate
and puerile ?	Had she studied so long
in the school of adversity, without conviction of the duty of a virtuous inde-
pendence ?	Was she not a rational be-
ing, fully imbued with the justice of her
cause ?	Was it not ignoble to refuse the
province of a vindicator of the injured,
before any tribunal, however tremendous
or unjust ?	And who was Ormond, that
his eye should inspire terror ?

The father or brother of Helena might assume the office without indecorum. Nay, a mother or sister might not be debarred from it. Why then should she, who was actuated by equal zeal, and was engaged by ties stronger than consanguinity in the promotion of her friend's happiness. It is true she did not view the subject in the light in which it was commonly viewed by brothers and parents. It was not a gust of rage that should transport her into his presence. She did not go to awaken his slumbering conscience, and to abash him in the pride of guilty triumph, but to rectify deliberate errors, and to change his course by the change of his principles. It was her business to point out to him the road of duty and happiness, from which he had strayed with no sinister intentions. This was to be done without raving and fury; but with amicable soberness, and in the way of calm and rational remonstrance. Yet there were scruples that would not be shut out,

and continually whispered to her—What
an office is this for a girl and a stranger
to assume !

In what manner should it be performed ? Should an interview be sought, and
her ideas be explained without confusion
or faltering, undismayed by ludicrous
airs or insolent frowns ? But this was a
point to be examined. Was Ormond
capable of such behaviour ? If he were,
it would be useless to attempt the refor-
mation of his errors. Such a man is incurable and obdurate. Such a man is
not to be sought as the husband of Helena ; but this surely is a different being.

The medium through which she had
viewed his character was an ample one,
but might not be very accurate. The
treatment which Helena had received from
him, exclusive of his fundamental error,
betokened a mind to which she did not
disdain to be allied. In spite of his defects, she saw that their elements were
more congenial, and the points of con-

tract, between this person and herself,
more numerous than between her and
Helena, whose voluptuous sweetness of
temper and mediocrity of understanding
excited in her bosom no genuine sympathy.

Every thing is progressive in the human
mind. When there is leisure to reflect,
ideas will succeed each other in a long
train, before the ultimate point be gained.
The attention must shift from one side to
the other of a given question, many times
before it settles. Constantia did not form
her resolutions in haste; but when once
formed, they were exempt from fluctuation. She reflected before she acted, and
therefore acted with consistency and vigour. She did not apprise her friend of
her intention. She was willing that she
should benefit by her interposition, before she knew it was employed.

She sent her Lucy with a note to Ormond's house. It was couched in these
terms:

"Constance Dudley requests an interview with Mr. Ormond. Her business being of some moment, she wishes him to name an hour when most disengaged."

An answer was immediately returned, that at three o'clock, in the afternoon, he should be glad to see her.

This message produced no small surprise in Ormond. He had not withdrawn his notice from Constance, and had marked, with curiosity and approbation, the progress of the connexion between the two women. The impressions which he had received from the report of Helena were not dissimilar to those which Constance had imbibed from the same quarter respecting himself; but he gathered from them no suspicion of the purpose of a visit. He recollected his connexion with Craig. This lady had had an opportunity of knowing that some connexion subsisted between them. He concluded that some information or inquiry respecting Craig might occasion this event. As

it was, it gave him considerable satisfaction. It would enable him more closely
to examine one, with respect to whom
he-entertained great curiosity.

Ormond's conjecture was partly right.
Constantia did not forget her having
traced Craig to this habitation. She designed to profit by the occasion which
this circumstance afforded her, of making some inquiry respecting Craig, in
order to introduce, by suitable degrees,
a more important subject.

The appointed hour having arrived,
he received her in his drawing-room. He
knew what was due to his guest. He
loved to mortify, by his negligence, the
pride of his equals and superiors, but a
lower class had nothing to fear from his
insolence. Constantia took the seat that
was offered to her, without speaking.
She had made suitable preparations for
this interview, and her composure was
invincible. The manners of her host
were by no means calculated to discon-

cort her. His air was conciliating and
attentive.

She began with naming Craig, as one
known to Ormond, and desired to be informed of his place of abode. She was
proceeding to apologize for this request,
by explaining in general terms, that her
father's infirmities prevented him from
acting for himself, that Craig was his
debtor to a large amount, that he stood
in need of all that justly belonged to
him, and was in pursuit of some means
of tracing Craig to his retreat. Ormond
interrupted her, examining, at the same
time, with a vigilance somewhat too un-
sparing, the effects which his words
should produce upon her.

You may spare yourself the trouble of
explaining. I am acquainted with the
whole affair between Craig and your family. He has concealed from me nothing. I know *all* that has passed between you.

In saying this, Ormond intended that

his looks and emphasis should convey his full meaning. In the style of her comments he saw none of those corroborating symptoms that he expected.

Indeed! He has been very liberal of his confidence. Confession is a token of penitence, but, alas! I fear he has deceived you. To be sincere was doubtless his true interest; but he is too much in the habit of judging superficially. If he has told you all, there is, indeed, no need of explanation. This visit is, in that case, sufficiently accounted for. Is it in your power, Sir, to inform us whither he has gone?

For what end should I tell you? I promise you you will not follow him. Take my word for it, he is totally unworthy of you. Let the past be no precedent for the future. If you have not made that discovery yourself, I have made it for you. I expect at least to be thanked for my trouble.

This speech was unintelligible to Con-

stance.   Her looks betokened a perplexi-
ty unmingled with fear or shame.

It is my way, continued he; to say
what I think.   I care little for consequences.   I have said that I know *all*.
This will excuse me for being perfectly
explicit.   That I am mistaken is very
possible ; but I am inclined to place that
matter beyond the reach of a doubt.   Listen to me, and confirm me in the opinion
I have already formed of your good sense,
by viewing, in a just light, the unreserv-
edness with which you are treated.   I
have something to tell, which, if you are
wise, you will not be offended at my telling so roundly.   On the contrary you will
thank me, and perceive that my conduct
is a proof of my respect for you.   The
person whom you met here is named
Craig, but, as he tells me, is not the
man you look for.   This man's brother,
the partner of your father, and, as he
assured me, your own accepted and illi-
citly gratified lover, is dead.

These words were uttered without any
extenuating hesitation or depression of
tone. On the contrary, the most offen-
sive terms were drawn out in the most
deliberate and emphatic manner. Constantia's cheeks glowed, and her eyes
sparkled with indignation, but she forbore to interrupt. The looks with which
she listened to the remainder of the
speech shewed that she fully compre-
hended the scene, and enabled him to
comprehend it. He proceeded.

This man is a brother of that. Their
resemblance in figure occasioned your
mistake. Your father's debtor died, it
seems, on his arrival at Jamaica. There
he met with this brother, and bequeathed
to him his property and papers. Some
of these papers are in my possession.
They are letters from Constantia Dudley,
and are parts of an intrigue, which, con-
sidering the character of the man, was
not much to her honour. Such was this
man's narrative told to me some time be-

fore your meeting with him at his house.
I have a right to judge in this affair, that
is, I have a right to my opinion. If I
mistake, and I half suspect myself, you
are able, perhaps, to rectify my error,
and in a case like this doubtless you will
not want the inclination.

Perhaps if the countenance of this man
had not been characterized by the keenest
intelligence, and a sort of careless and
overflowing good-will, this speech might
have produced different effects. She was
prepared, though imperfectly, for entering into his character. He waited for
an answer, which she gave without emotion.

You are deceived. I am sorry for your
own sake that you are. He must have
had some end in view in imposing these
falsehoods upon you, which, perhaps,
they have enabled him to accomplish.
As to myself, this man can do me no injury. I willingly make you my judge.
The letters you speak of will alone suf-

fice to my vindication. They never were received from me, and are forgeries. That man always persisted till he made himself the dupe of his own artifices. That incident in his plot, on the introduction of which he probably the most applauded himself, will most powerfully operate to defeat it.

Those letters never were received from me, and are forgeries. His skill in imitation extended no farther in the present case than my hand-writing. My modes of thinking and expression were beyond the reach of his mimicry.

When she had finished, Ormond spent a moment in ruminating. I perceive you are right, said he. I suppose he has purloined from me two hundred guineas which I entrusted to his fidelity. And yet I received a letter:—but that may likewise be a forgery. By my soul, continued he, in a tone that had more of satisfaction than disappointment in it, this fellow was an adept at his trade. I do not repine. I have bought the exhibition at a cheap rate. The pains that he took did not merit a less recompense. I am glad that he was contented with so little. Had he persisted he might have raised the price far above its value. 'Twill be lamentable if he receive more than he stipulated for; if, in his last purchase, the gallows should be thrown into the bargain. May he have the wisdom to see that a halter, though not included in his terms, is only a new instance of his good fortune: but his cunning will hardly carry him thus far. His stupidity will, no doubt, prefer a lingering to a sudden exit.

But this man and his destiny are trifles. Let us leave them to themselves. Your name is Constance. 'Twas given you I suppose that you might be known by it. Pr'ythee, Constance, was this the only purpose that brought you hither? If it were, it has received as ample a discussion as it merits. You *came for* this end, but will remain, I hope, for a better one. Having dismissed Craig and his plots, let us now talk of each other.

I confess, said the lady, with an hesitation she could not subdue, this was not my only purpose. One much more important has produced this visit.

Indeed! pray let me know it. I am glad that so trivial an object as Craig did not occupy the first place in your thoughts. Proceed I beseech you.

It is a subject on which I cannot enter without hesitation. An hesitation unworthy of me.——

Stop, cried Ormond, rising and touching the bell, nothing like time to make a conquest of embarrassment. We will. defer this conference six minutes, just while we eat our dinner.

At the same moment a servant entered, with two plates and the usual apparatus for dinner. On seeing this she rose in some hurry to depart. I thought, sir,

you were disengaged. I will call at
some other hour.

He seized her hand, and held her from
going, but with an air by no means dis-
respectful. Nay, said he, what is it that
scares you away? Are you terrified at
the mention of victuals? You must have
fasted long when it comes to that. I told
you true. I am disengaged, but not from
the obligation of eating and drinking.
No doubt *you* have dined. No reason
why *I* should go without my dinner. If
you do not chuse to partake with me, so
much the better. Your temperance
ought to dispense with two meals in an
hour. Be a looker-on, or, if that will
not do, retire into my library, where,
in six minutes, I will be with you, and
lend you my aid in the arduous task of
telling me what you came with an intention of telling.

This singular address disconcerted and
abashed her. She was contented to follow the servant silently into an adjoin-

ing apartment Here she reflected with
no small surprise on the behaviour of
this man. Though ruffled, she was not
heartily displeased with it. She had
scarcely time to recollect herself, when
he entered. He immediately seated her,
and himself opposite to her. He fixed
his eyes without scruple on her face. His
gaze was stedfast, but not insolent or
oppressive. He surveyed her with the
looks with which he would have eyed a
charming portrait. His attention was
occupied with what he saw, as that of
an artist is occupied when viewing a
madonna of Raphael. At length he broke
silence.

At dinner I was busy in thinking what
it was you had to disclose. I will not
fatigue you with my guesses. They
would be impertinent, as long as the truth
is going to be disclosed—He paused, and
then continued: but I see you cannot
dispense with my aid. Perhaps your
business relates to Helena. She has

done wrong, and you wish me to rebuke
the girl.

Constantia profited by this opening,
and said, Yes, she has done wrong. It
is true my business relates to her. I came
hither as a suppliant in her behalf. Will
you not assist her in recovering the path
from which she has deviated? She left it
from confiding more in the judgment of
her guide than her own. There is one
method of repairing the evil. It lies with
you to repair that evil.

During this address the gaiety of Ormond disappeared. He fixed his eyes on
Constance with new and even pathetic
earnestness. I guessed as much, said he.
I have often been deceived in my judgment of characters. Perhaps I do not
comprehend your's: yet it is not little
that I have heard respecting you. Something I have seen. I begin to suspect a
material error in my theory of human
nature. Happy will it be for Helena if
my suspicions be groundless.

You are Helena's friend. Be mine also, and advise me. Shall I marry this girl or not? You know on what terms we live. Are they suitable to our respective characters? Shall I wed this girl, or shall things remain as they are?

I have an irreconcilable aversion to a sad brow and a sick bed. Helena is grieved, because her neighbours sneer and point at her. So far she is a fool, but that is a folly of which she never will be cured. Marriage, it seems, will set all right. Answer me, Constance, shall I marry?

There was something in the tone, but more in the tenor of this address that startled her. There was nothing in this man but what came upon her unaware. This sudden effusion of confidence was particularly unexpected and embarrassing. She scarcely knew whether to regard it as serious or a jest. On observing her indisposed to speak, he continued:

Away with these impertinent circuities
and scruples. I know your meaning.
Why should I pretend ignorance, and
put you to the trouble of explanation?
You came hither with no other view
than to exact this question, and furnish
an answer. Why should not we come at
once to the point? I have for some time
been dubious on this head. There is
something wanting to determine the balance. If you have that something,
throw it into the proper scale.

You err if you think this manner of
addressing you is wild or improper. This
girl is the subject of discourse. If she
was not to be so, why did you favour me
with this visit? You have sought me,
and introduced yourself. I have, in like
manner, overlooked ordinary forms; a
negligence that has been systematic with
me; but, in the present case, particularly justifiable by your example. Shame
upon you, presumptuous girl, to suppose
yourself the only rational being among

mankind. And yet, if you thought so, why did you thus unceremoniously intrude upon my retirements? This act is of a piece with the rest. It shews you to be one whose existence I did not believe possible.

Take care. You know not what you have done. You came hither as Helena's friend. Perhaps time may shew that in this visit you have performed the behest of her bitterest enemy. But that is out of season. This girl is our mutual property. You are her friend; I am her lover. Her happiness is precious in my eyes and in your's. To the rest of mankind she is a noisome weed, that cannot be shunned too cautiously, nor trampled on too much. If we forsake her, infamy that is now kept at bay will seize upon her, and while it mangles her form, will tear from her her innocence. She has no arms with which to contend against that foe. Marriage will place her at once in security. Shall it be? You have

an exact knowledge of her strength and
her weakness. Of me you know little.
Perhaps, before that question can be satisfactorily answered, it is requisite to
know the qualities of her husband. Be
my character henceforth the subject of
your study. I will furnish you with all
the light in my power. Be not hasty in
deciding, but when your decision is
formed, let me know it.

He waited for an answer, which she,
at length, summoned resolution enough
to give.

You have come to the chief point
which I had in view in making this visit.
To say truth, I came hither to remon-
strate with you on withholding that which
Helena may justly claim from you. Her
happiness will be unquestionably restored,
and increased by it. Your's will not be
impaired. Matrimony will not produce
any essential change in your situation.
It will produce no greater or different
intercourse than now exists. Helena is

on the brink of a gulf which I shudder
to look upon. I believe that you will
not injure yourself by snatching her from
it. I am sure that you will confer an inexpressible benefit upon her. Let me then
persuade you to do her and yourself
justice.

No persuasion, said Ormond, after recovering from a fit of thoughtfulness, is
needful for this end ; I only want to be
convinced. You have decided, but I
fear hastily. By what inscrutable influences are our steps guided. Come, proceed in your exhortations. Argue with
the utmost clearness and cogency. Arm
yourself with all the irresistibles of eloquence. Yet you are building nothing.
You are only demolishing. Your argument is one thing ; its tendency is another ; and is the reverse of all you expect and desire. My assent will be refused with an obstinacy proportioned to
the force that you exert to obtain it, and
to the just application of that force.

I see, replied the lady, smiling and leaving her seat, you can talk in riddles, as well as other people. This visit has been too long. I shall, indeed, be sorry, if my interference, instead of serving my friend, has injured her. I have acted an uncommon, and, as it may seem, an ambiguous part. I shall be contented with construing my motives in my own way. I wish you a good evening.

'Tis false, cried he, sternly, you do not wish it.

How? exclaimed the astonished Constance.

I will put your sincerity to the test. Allow me to spend this evening in your company: then it will be well spent, and I shall believe your wishes sincere: else, continued he, changing his affected austerity into a smile, Constance is a liar.

You are a singular man. I hardly know how to understand you.

Well. Words are made to carry

meanings. You shall have them in abundance. Your house is your citadel. I will not enter it without leave. Permit me to visit it when I please. But that is too much. It is more than I would allow you. When will you permit me to visit you?

I cannot answer when I do not understand. You cloathe your thoughts in a garb so uncouth, that I know not in what light they are to be viewed.

Well, now, I thought you understood my language, and were an English-woman, but I will use another. Shall I have the honour (bowing with a courtly air of supplication) of occasionally paying my respects to you at your own dwelling? It would be cruel to condemn those who have the happiness of knowing Miss Dudley to fashionable restraints. At what hour will she be least incommoded by a visitant?

I am as little pleased with formalities, replied the lady, as you are. My friends

I cannot see too often. They need to consult merely their own convenience. Those who are not my friends I cannot see too seldom. You have only to establish your title to that name, and your welcome at all times is sure. Till then you must not look for it.

CHAP. VI.

HERE ended this conference. She had
by no means suspected the manner in
which it would be conducted. All punc-
tilios were trampled under foot by the
impetuosity of Ormond. Things were,
at once, and without delay, placed upon
a certain footing. The point, which ordinary persons would have employed
months in attaining, was reached in a
moment. While these incidents were
fresh in her memory, they were accompanied with a sort of trepidation, the
offspring at once of pleasure and surprise.

Ormond had not deceived her expectations, but hearsay and personal examination, however uniform their testimony
may be, produce a very different impression. In her present reflections, Helena

and her lover approached to the front of the stage, and were viewed with equal perspicuity. One consequence of this was, that their characters were more powerfully contrasted with each other, and the eligibility of marriage appeared not quite so incontestible as before.

Was not equality implied in this compact ? Marriage is an instrument of pleasure or pain in proportion as this equality is more or less. What, but the fascination of his senses is it, that ties Ormond to Helena. Is this a basis on which marriage may properly be built ?

If things had not gone thus far, the impropriety of marriage could not be doubted ; but at present there is a choice of evils, and that may now be desirable, which at a former period, and in different circumstances, would have been clearly otherwise.

The evils of the present connection are known ; those of marriage are future and contingent. Helena cannot be the object of a genuine and lasting passion; another may; this is not merely possible; nothing is more likely to happen: this event, therefore, ought to be included in our calculation. There would be a material deficiency without it. What was the amount of the misery that would in this case ensue.

Constantia was qualified beyond most others to form an adequate conception of this misery. One of the ingredients in her character was a mild and stedfast enthusiasm. Her sensibilities to social pleasure, and her conceptions of the benefits to flow from the conformity and concurrence of intentions and wishes, heightening and refining the sensual passion, were exquisite.

There indeed were evils, the foresight of which tended to prevent them, but was there wisdom in creating obstacles in the way of a suitable alliance. Before we act, we must consider not only the misery.

produced, but the happiness precluded by
our measures.

In no case, perhaps, is the decision of
a human being impartial, or totally uninfluenced by sinister and selfish motives.
If Constantia surpassed others, it was
not because her motives were pure, but
because they possessed more of purity
than those of others. Sinister considerations flow in upon us through impercep-
tible channels, and modify our thoughts
in numberless ways, without our being
truly conscious of their presence. Constance was young, and her heart was open
at a thousand pores, to the love of excellence. The image of Ormond occupied
the chief place in her fancy, and was
endowed with attractive and venerable
qualities. A bias was hence created that
swayed her thoughts, though she knew
not that they were swayed. To this
might justly be imputed some part of
that reluctance which she now felt to give

Ormond to Helena. But this was not
sufficient to turn the scale. That which
had previously mounted was indeed
heavier than before; but this addition
did not enable it to outweigh its opposite.
Marriage was still the best upon the
whole, but her heart was tortured to
think that, best as it was, it abounded
with so many evils.

On the evening of the next day Ormond entered with careless abruptness
Constantia's sitting-room. He was introduced to her father. A general and
unrestrained conversation immediately
took place. Ormond addressed Mr.
Dudley with the familiarity of an old
acquaintance. In three minutes all embarrassment was discarded. The lady
and her visitant were accurate observers
of each other. In the remarks of the
latter, and his vein was an abundant one,
there was a freedom and originality alto-
gether new to his hearers. In his easiest
and sprightliest sallies were tokens of a

mind habituated to profound and extensive views. His associations were formed
on a comprehensive scale.

He pretended to nothing, and studied
the concealments of ambiguity more in
reality than in appearance. Constantia,
however, discovered a sufficient resemblance between their theories of virtue
and duty. The difference between them
lay in the inferences arbitrarily deduced,
and in which two persons may vary without end, and yet never be repugnant.
Constantia delighted her companion by
the facility with which she entered into
his meaning, the sagacity she displayed
in drawing out his hints, circumscribing
his conjectures, and thwarting or quali-
fying his maxims. The scene was generally replete with ardour and contention,
and yet the impression left on the mind
of Ormond was full of harmony. Her
discourse tended to rouse him from his
lethargy, to furnish him with powerful
excitements, and the time spent in her

company seemed like a doubling of existence.

The comparison could not but suggest itself, between this scene and that exhibited by Helena. With the latter, voluptuous blandishments, musical prattle, and silent but expressive homage, composed a banquet delicious for a while, but whose sweetness now began to pall upon his taste. It supplied him with no new ideas, and hindered him, by the lulling sensations it inspired, from profiting by his former acquisitions. Helena was beautiful. Apply the scale, and not a member was found inelegantly disposed, or negligently moulded. Not a curve that was blemished by an angle or ruffled by asperities. The irradiations of her eyes were able to dissolve the knottiest fibres, and their azure was serene beyond any that nature had elsewhere exhibited. Over the rest of her form the glistening and rosy hues were diffused with prodigal luxuriance, and mingled in endless

and wanton variety. Yet this image had
fewer attractions even to the senses than
that of Constance. So great is the difference between forms animated by different degrees of intelligence.

The interviews of Ormond and Constance grew more frequent. The progress which they made in the knowledge
of each other was rapid. Two positions
that were favourite ones with him were
quickly subverted. He was suddenly
changed, from being one of the calum-
niators of the female sex, to one of its
warmest eulogists. This was a point on
which Constantia had ever been a vigorous disputant; but her arguments, in
their direct tendency, would never have
made a convert of this man. Their force,
intrinsically considered, was nothing. He
drew his conclusions from incidental circumstances. Her reasonings might be
fallacious or valid, but they were so composed, arranged, and delivered; were
drawn from such sources, and ac-

companied with such illustrations, as
plainly testified a manlike energy in the
reasoner. In this indirect and circuitous
way her point was unanswerably established.

Your reasoning is bad, he would say :
every one of your conclusions is false.
Not a single allegation but may be easily
confuted ; and yet I allow that your position is incontrovertibly proved by them.
How bewildered is that man who never
thinks for himself! who rejects a principle merely because the arguments brought
in support of it are insufficient. I must
not reject the truth because another has
unjustifiably adopted it. I want to reach
a certain hill-top. Another has reached
it before me, but the ladder he used is
too weak to bear me. What then ? Am
I to stay below on that account ? No :
I have only to construct one suitable to
the purpose, and of strength sufficient.

A second maxim had never been confuted till now. It inculcated the insig-

nificance and hollowness of love. No pleasure he thought was to be despised for its own sake. Every thing was good in its place, but amorous gratifications were to be degraded to the bottom of the catalogue The enjoyments of music and landscape were of a much higher order. Epicurism itself was entitled to more respect. Love, in itself, was in his opinion of little worth, and only of importance as the source of the most terrible of intellectual maladies. Sexual sensations associating themselves, in a certain way, with our ideas, beget a disease which has indeed found no place in the catalogue, but is a case of more entire subversion and confusion of mind than any other. The victim is callous to the sentiments of honour and shame, insensible to the most palpable distinctions of right and wrong, a systematic opponent of testimony, and obstinate perverter of truth.

Ormond was partly right. Madness like death can be averted by no foresight or previous contrivance. This probably is one of its characteristics. He that witnesses its influence on another with most horror, and most fervently deprecates its ravages, is not therefore more safe. This circumstance was realized in the history of Ormond.

This infatuation, if it may be so called, was gradual in its progress. The sensations which Helena was now able to excite were of a new kind. Her power was not merely weakened, but her endeavours counteracted their own end. Her fondness was rejected with disdain, or borne with reluctance. The lady was not slow in perceiving this change. The stroke of death would have been more acceptable. His own reflections were too tormenting to make him willing to discuss them in words. He was not aware of the effects produced by this change in his demeanour, till informed of it by herself.

One evening he displayed symptoms of

uncommon dissatisfaction. Her tenderness was unable to dispel it. He complained of want of sleep. This afforded
a hint, which she drew forth in one of
her enchanting ditties. Habit had almost
conferred upon her the power of spontaneous poesy, and while she pressed his
forehead to her bosom, she warbled forth
a strain airy and exuberant in numbers,
tender and ecstatic in its imagery.

Sleep, extend thy downy pinion,
   Hasten from thy cell with speed;
Spread around thy soft dominion;
   Much those brows thy balmy presence need.

Wave thy wand of slumberous power,
   Moistened in Lethean dews,
To charm the busy spirits of the hour,
   And brighten memory's malignant hues.

Thy mantle, dark and starless, cast
   Over my selected youth;
Bury in thy womb the mournful past,
   And soften with thy dreams th' asperities of
     truth.

The changeful hues of his impassioned sleep,
My office it shall be to watch the while;
With thee, my love, when fancy prompts, to weep,
And when thou smil'st, to smile.

But sleep! I charge thee, visit not these eyes,
Nor raise thy dark pavilion here,
'Till morrow from the cave of ocean rise,
And whisper tuneful joy in nature's ear,

But mutely let me lie, and sateless gaze
At all the soul that in his visage sits,
While spirits of harmonious air——

Here her voice sunk, and the line terminated in a sigh. Her museful ardours were chilled by the looks of Ormond. Absorbed in his own thoughts, he appeared scarcely to attend to this strain. His sternness was proof against her accustomed fascinations. At length she pathetically complained of his coldness, and insinuated her suspicions, that his affection was transferred to another object. He started from her embrace, and after two or three turns across the room, he

stood before her. His large eyes were
stedfastly fixed upon her face.

Aye, said he, thou hast guessed right.
The love, poor as it was, that I had for
thee is gone: henceforth thou art desolate indeed. Would to God thou wert
wise. Thy woes are but beginning; I
fear they will terminate fatally; if so,
the catastrophe cannot come too quickly.

I disdain to appeal to thy justice, Helena, to remind thee of conditions so-
lemnly and explicitly assumed. Shall
thy blood be upon thy own head? No.
I will bear it myself. Though the load
would crush a mountain, I will bear it.

I cannot help it; I make not myself;
I am moulded by circumstances: whether
I shall love thee or not is no longer in
my own choice. Marriage is, indeed,
still in my power. I may give thee my
name, and share with thee my fortune.
Will these content thee? Thou canst not
partake of my love. Thou canst have
no part in my tenderness. These are re-

served for another more worthy than
thou.

But no ; thy state is to the last degree forlorn : even marriage is denied
thee. Thou wast contented to take me
without it ; to dispense with the name of
wife ; but the being who has displaced
thy image in my heart is of a different
class. She will be to me a wife, or nothing ; and I must be her husband, or
perish.

Do not deceive thyself, Helena. I
know what it is in which thou hast placed
thy felicity. Life is worth retaining by
thee but on one condition. I know the
incurableness of thy infirmity ; but be
not deceived. Thy happiness is ravished
from thee. The condition on which thou
consentest to live is annulled. I love
thee no longer.

No truth was ever more delicious ;
none was ever more detestable. I fight
against conviction, and I cling to it. That
I love thee no longer is at once a sub-

ject of joy and of mourning. I struggle
to believe thee superior to this shock;
that thou wilt be happy though deserted
by me. Whatever be thy destiny, my
reason will not allow me to be miserable
on that account: yet I would give the
world; I would forfeit every claim but
that which I hope upon the heart of Constance, to be sure that thy tranquillity
will survive this stroke.

But let come what will, look no longer
to me for offices of love. Henceforth all
intercourse of tenderness ceases. Perhaps all personal intercourse whatever.
But though this good be refused, thou
art sure of independence. I will guard
thy ease and thy honour with a father's
scrupulousness. Would to heaven a sister
could be created by adoption. I am
willing, for thy sake, to be an imposter.
I will own thee to the world for my sister,
and carry thee whither the cheat shall
never be detected. I would devote my
whole life to prevarication and falsehood

for thy sake, if that would suffice to make
thee happy.

To this speech Helena had nothing to
answer: her sobs and tears choaked
all utterance. She hid her face with
her handkerchief, and sat powerless and
overwhelmed with despair. Ormond
traversed the room uneasily; sometimes
moving to and fro with quick steps,
sometimes standing and eyeing her with
looks of compassion. At length he
spoke.

' It is time to leave you. This is the
first night that you will spend in dreary
solitude. I know it will be sleepless
and full of agony; but the sentence
cannot be recalled. Henceforth regard
me as a brother. I will prove myself
one. All other claims are swallowed
up in a superior affection.—In saying
this, he left the house, and almost without intending it, found himself in a few
minutes at Mr. Dudley's door.

CHAP. VII.

THE politeness of Melbourne had somewhat abated Mr. Dudley's aversion to society. He allowed himself sometimes to comply with urgent invitations. On this evening he happened to be at the house of that gentleman. Ormond entered, and found Constantia alone. An interview of this kind was seldom enjoyed, though earnestly wished for by Constantia, who was eager to renew the subject of her first conversation with Ormond. I have already explained the situation of her mind. All her wishes were concentred in the marriage of Helena. The eligibility of this scheme, in every view which she took of it, appeared in a stronger light. She was not aware that any new obstacle had arisen. She was free from the consciousness of any secret bias. Much less did her modesty suspect that she herself would prove an insuperable impediment to this plan.

There was more than usual solemnity in Ormond's demeanour. After he was seated he continued, contrary to his custom, to be silent. These singularities were not unobserved by Constance. They did not, however, divert her from her purpose.

I am glad to see you, said she. We so seldom enjoy the advantage of a private interview. I have much to say to you. You authorize me to deliberate on your actions, and in some measure to prescribe to you. This is a province which I hope to discharge with integrity and diligence. I am convinced that Helena's happiness and your own can be secured in one way only. I will emulate your candour, and come at once to the point. Why have you delayed so long the justice that is due to this helpless and

lovely girl? There are a thousand reasons why you should think of no other
alternative. You have been pleased to
repose some degree of confidence in my
judgment. Hear my full and deliberate
opinion. Make Helena your wife. This
is the unequivocal prescription of your
duty.

This address was heard by Ormond
without surprise; but his countenance
betrayed the acuteness of his feelings.
The bitterness that overflowed his heart
was perceptible in his tone when he
spoke.

Most egregiously are you deceived.
Such is the line with which human capacity presumes to fathom futurity. With
all your discernment you do not see that
marriage would effectually destroy me.
You do not see that, whether beneficial
or otherwise in its effects, marriage is
impossible. You are merely prompting
me to suicide; but how shall I inflict
the wound? Where is the weapon? See

you not that I am powerless? Leap, say you, into the flames. See you not that I am fettered? Will a mountain move at your bidding? Sooner than I in the path which you prescribe to me.

This speech was inexplicable. She pressed him to speak less enigmatically. Had he formed his resolution? If so, arguments and remonstrances were superfluous. Without noticing her interrogatories, he continued:

I am too hasty in condemning you. You judge, not against, but without knowledge. When sufficiently informed, your decision will be right. Yet how can you be ignorant? Can you for a moment contemplate yourself and me, and not perceive an insuperable bar to this union?

You place me, said Constantia, in a very disagreeable predicament. I have not deserved this treatment from you. This is an unjustifiable deviation from plain dealing. Of what impediment do

you speak. I can safely say that I know
of none.

Well, resumed he, with augmented
eagerness, I must supply you with knowledge. I repeat, that I perfectly rely on
the rectitude of your judgment. Sum-
mon all your sagacity and disinterested-
ness and choose for me. You know in
what light Helena has been viewed by
me. I have ceased to view her in this
light. She has become an object of indifference: nay, I am not certain that I
do not hate her. Not indeed for her own
sake, but because I love another. Shall
marry her whom I hate, when there
exists one whom I love with unconquer-
able ardour?

Constantia was thunderstruck at this
intelligence. She looked at him with
some expression of doubt. How is this?
said she. Why did you not tell me this
before?

When I last talked with you on this
subject I knew it not myself. It has oc-

curred since. I have seized the first occasion that has offered to inform you of it. Say now, since such is my condition, ought Helena to be my wife?

Constantia was silent. Her heart bled for what she foresaw would be the sufferings and forlorn destiny of Helena. She had not courage to inquire further into this new engagement.

I wait for your answer, Constance. Shall I defraud myself of all the happiness that would accrue from a match of inclination? Shall I put fetters on my usefulness? This is the style in which you speak. Shall I preclude all the good to others that would flow from a suitable alliance? Shall I abjure the woman I love, and marry her whom I hate?

Hatred, replied the lady, is a harsh word. Helena has not deserved that you should hate her. I own this is a perplexing circumstance. It would be wrong to determine hastily. Suppose you give yourself to Helena, will more

than yourself be injured by it? Who is
this lady? Will she be rendered unhappy
by a determination in favour of another?
This is a point of the utmost importance.

At these words Ormond forsook his
seat, and advanced close up to Constantia. You say true. This is a point of
inexpressible importance. It would be
presumption in me to decide. That is
the lady's own province. And now, say
truly, are you willing to accept Ormond
with all his faults? Who but yourself
could be mistress of all the springs of my
soul? I know the sternness of your pro-
bity. This discovery will only make
you more strenuously the friend of Helena. Yet why should you not shun
either extreme? Lay yourself out of
view. And yet, perhaps the happiness
of Constance is not unconcerned in this
question. Is there no part of me in
which you discover your own likeness?
Am I deceived, or is it an incontroulable
destiny that unites us?

This declaration was truly unexpected by Constance. She gathered from it nothing but excitements of grief. After some pause she said :—This appeal to me has made no change in my opinion. I still think that justice requires you to become the husband of Helena. As to me, do you think my happiness rests upon so slight a foundation? I cannot love but when my understanding points out to me the propriety of love. Ever since I have known you I have looked upon you as rightfully belonging to another. Love could not take place in my circumstances. Yet I will not conceal from you my sentiments. I am not sure that in different circumstances I should not have loved. I am acquainted with your worth. I do not look for a faultless man. I have met with none whose blemishes were fewer.

It matters not, however, what I should have been. I cannot interfere, in this case, with the claims of my friend. I

have no passion to struggle with. I
hope in every vicissitude to enjoy your
esteem, and nothing more. There is but
one way in which mine can be secured,
and that is by espousing this unhappy
girl.

No, exclaimed Ormond. Require not
impossibilities. Helena can never be any
thing to me. I should with unspeakably
more willingness assail my own life.

What, said the lady, will Helena
think of this sudden and dreadful change?
I cannot bear to think upon the feelings
that this information will excite.

She knows it already. I have this moment left her. I explained to her in a few
words my motives, and assured her of
my unalterable resolution. I have vow-
ed never to see her more but as a brother,
and this vow she has just heard.

Constantia could not suppress her astonishment and compassion at this intelligence. No surely, you could not be so
cruel! And this was done with your

usual abruptness, I suppose. Precipi-
tate and implacable man! Cannot you
foresee the effects of this madness? You
have planted a dagger in her heart.
You have disappointed me. I did not
think you could act so inhumanly.

Nay, beloved Constance, be not so liberal of your reproaches. Would you
have me deceive her? She must shortly
have known it. Could the truth be told
too soon?

Much too soon, replied the lady, fervently. I have always condemned the
maxims by which you act. Your scheme
is headlong and barbarous. Could not
you regard with some little compassion
that love that sacrificed for your unworthy sake honest fame and the peace of
virtue? Is she not a poor outcast, goaded
by compunction, and hooted at by a malignant and misjudging world, and who
was it that reduced her to this deplorable
condition? For whose sake did she willingly consent to brave evils, by which

the stoutest heart is appalled? Did this
argue no greatness of mind? Who ever
surpassed her in fidelity and tenderness?
But thus has she been rewarded.   I
shudder to think what may be the event.
Her courage cannot possibly support her
against treatment so harsh; so perversely
and wantonly cruel. Heaven grant that
you are not shortly made bitterly to la-
ment this rashness.

Ormond was penetrated with these reproaches.   They persuaded him for a
moment that his deed was wrong; that
he had not unfolded his intentions to Helena with a suitable degree of gentleness
and caution. Little more was said on
this occasion. Constantia exhorted him,
in the most earnest and pathetic manner,
to return and recant, or extenuate his
former declarations. He could not be
brought to promise compliance. When
he parted from her, however, he was
half resolved to act as she advised. Solitary reflection made him change this

resolution, and he returned to his own house.

During the night he did little else than ruminate on the events of the preceding evening. He entertained little doubt of his ultimate success with Constance. She gratified him in nothing, but left him every thing to hope. She had hitherto it seems regarded him with indifference, but this had been sufficiently explained. That conduct would be pursued, and that passion be entertained, which her judgment should previously approve. What then was the obstacle? It originated in the claims of Helena; but what were these claims? It was fully ascertained that he should never be united to this girl. If so, the end contemplated by Constance, and for the sake of which only his application was rejected, could never be obtained. Unless her rejection of him could procure a husband for her friend, it would, on her own principles, be improper and superfluous.

What was to be done with Helena?
It was a terrible alternative to which he
was reduced—to marry her or see her
perish. But was this alternative quite
sure? Could not she, by time or by ju-
dicious treatment, be reconciled to her
lot? It was to be feared that he had not
made a suitable beginning: and yet,
perhaps it was most expedient that an
hasty and abrupt sentence should be suc-
ceeded by forbearance and lenity. He
regretted his precipitation, and though
unused to the melting mood, tears were
wrung from him by the idea of the misery which he had probably occasioned.
He was determined to repair his misconduct as speedily as possible, and to pay
her a conciliating visit the next morning.

He went early to her house: he was
informed by the servant that her mistress
had not yet risen. Was it usual, he
asked, for her to lie so late? No; he
was answered, she never knew it happen
before, but she supposed her mistress

was not well. She was just going into
her chamber to see what was the matter.

Why, said Ormond, do you suppose
that she is sick?

She was poorly last night. About nine
o'clock she sent out for some physic to
make her sleep.

To make her sleep! exclaimed Ormond, in a faltering and affrighted ac-
cent.

Yes, she said she wanted it for that;
so I went to the apothecary's. When I
came back she was very poorly indeed.
I asked her if I might not sit up with her.
No, she said, I do not want any body.
You may go to bed as soon as you please,
and tell Fabian to do the same. I shall
not want you again.

What did you buy?

Some kind of water; laudanum I think
they call it. She wrote it down, and I
carried the paper to Mr. Eckhart's, and
he gave it to me in a bottle, and I gave
it to my mistress.

'Tis well: retire: I will see how she is myself.

Ormond had conceived himself forti-
fied against every disaster: he looked
for nothing but evil, and therefore, in
ordinary cases, regarded its approach
without fear or surprise. Now, however,
he found that his tremors would not be
stilled: his perturbations increased with
every step that brought him nearer to
her chamber. He knocked, but no answer
was returned. He opened the door, advanced to the bed side, and drew back
the curtains. He shrunk from the spectacle that presented itself——Was this
the Helena that a few hours before was
blithsome with health and radiant with
beauty! Her visage was serene, but
sunken and pale. Death was in every
line of it. To his tremulous and hurried
scrutiny every limb was rigid and cold.

The habits of Ormond tended to obscure the appearances, if not to deaden
the emotions of sorrow. He was so

much accustomed to the frustration of well-intended efforts, and confided so much in his own integrity, that he was not easily disconcerted. He had merely to advert, on this occasion, to the tumultuous state of his feelings, in order to banish their confusion and restore himself to calm. Well, said he, as he dropped the curtain and turned towards another part of the room, this without doubt is a rueful spectacle. Can it be helped? Is there in man the power of recalling her? There is none such in me.

She is gone: well then, she *is* gone. If she were fool enough to die, I am not fool enough to follow her. I am determined to live and be happy notwithstanding. Why not?

Yet, this is a piteous sight. What is impossible to undo, might be easily prevented. A piteous spectacle! But what else, on an ampler scale, is the universe? Nature is a theatre of suffering. What

corner is unvisited by calamity and pain?
I have chosen as became me. I would
rather precede thee to the grave, than
live to be thy husband.

Thou hast done my work for me. Thou
hast saved thyself and me from a thousand evils. Thou hast acted as seemed
to thee best, and I am satisfied.

Hast thou decided erroneously? They
that know thee need not marvel at that.
Endless have been the proofs of thy
frailty. In favour of this last act something may be said: it is the last thou
wilt ever commit. Others only will experience its effects: thou hast at least
provided for thy own safety.

But what is here? A letter for me?
Had thy understanding been as prompt
as thy fingers, I could have borne with
thee. I can easily divine the contents of
this epistle.

He opened it, and found the tenor to
be as follows:

"You did not use, my dear friend, to

part with me in this manner. You never before treated me so roughly. I am, sorry, indeed I am, that I ever offended you. Could you suppose that I intended it? And if you knew that I meant not offence, why did you take offence?

"I am very unhappy, for I have lost you, my friend. You will never see me more, you say. That is very hard. I have deserved it to be sure, but I do not know how it has happened. Nobody more desired to please than I have done. Morning, noon, and night, it was my only study; but you will love me no more; you will see me no more. Forgive me, my friend, but I must say it is very hard.

"You said rightly; I do not wish to live without my friend. I have spent my life happily heretofore. 'Tis true, there have been transient uneasinesses, but your love was a reward and a cure for every thing. I desired nothing better in this world. Did you ever hear me

murmur? No: I was not so unjust. My
lot was happy, infinitely beyond my deserving. I merited not to be loved by
you. O that I had suitable words to
express my gratitude for your kindness!
but this last meeting—how different from
that which went before! Yet even then
there was something on your brow like
discontent, which I could not warble nor
whisper away as I used to do. But sad
as this was, it was nothing like the last.

"Could Ormond be so stern and so terrible? You knew that I would die, but
you need not have talked as if I were in
the way, and as if you had rather I should
die than live. But one thing I rejoice
at: I am a poor silly girl, but Constance
is a noble and accomplished one. Most
joyfully do I resign you to her, my dear
friend. You say you love her: she need
not be afraid of accepting you. There
will be no danger of your preferring another to her. It was very natural and
very right for you to prefer her to me.

She and you will be happy in each other.
It is this that sweetens the cup I am going to drink. Never did I go to sleep
with more good will than I now go to
death. Fare you well, my dear friend."

This letter was calculated to make a
deeper impression on Ormond than even
the sight of Helena's corpse. It was in
vain for some time that he endeavoured
to reconcile himself to this event. It
was seldom that he was able to forget it.
He was obliged to exert all his energies
to enable him to support the remembrance. The task was of course rendered easier by time.

It was immediately requisite to attend
to the disposal of the corpse. He felt
himself unfit for this mournful office.
He was willing to relieve himself from
it by any expedient. Helena's next neigh-
bour was an old lady, whose scruples
made her shun all direct intercourse with
this unhappy girl, yet she had performed
many acts of neighbourly kindness. She

readily obeyed the summons of Ormond,
on this occasion, to take charge of affairs
till another should assume it. Ormond
returned home, and sent the following
note to Constance.

"You have predicted aright. Helena
is dead. In a mind like your's every grief
will be suspended, and every regard absorbed in the attention due to the remains
of this unfortunate girl. I cannot attend
to them."

Constantia was extremely shocked by
this intelligence, but she was not un-
mindful of her duty. She prepared herself with mournful alacrity for the performance of it. Every thing that the
occasion demanded was done with diligence and care. Till this was accomplished, Ormond could not prevail upon
himself to appear upon the stage. He
was informed of this by a note from
Constance, who requested him to take
possession of the unoccupied dwelling and
its furniture.

Among the terms of his contract with Helena, Ormond had voluntarily inserted the exclusive property of a house and its furniture in this city, with funds adequate to her plentiful maintenance.— These he had purchased and transferred to her. To this he had afterwards added a rural retreat, in the midst of spacious and well-cultivated fields, three miles from Perth-Amboy, and seated on the right bank of the Sound. It is proper to mention that this farm was formerly the property of Mr. Dudley; had been fitted up by him, and used as his summer abode during his prosperity. In the division of his property it had fallen to one of his creditors, from whom it had been purchased by Ormond. This circumstance, in conjunction with the love which she bore to Constance, had suggested to Helena a scheme, which her want of foresight would, in different circumstances, have occasioned her to overlook. It was that of making her testament, by which

she bequeathed all that she possessed to
her friend. This was not done without
the knowledge and cheerful concurrence
of Ormond, who, together with Melbourne and another respectable citizen,
were named executors. 'Melbourne and
his friend were induced by their respect
for Constantia to consent to this nomi-
nation.

This had taken place before Ormond
and Constance had been introduced to
each other. After this event, Ormond
had sometimes been employed in contriv-
ing means for securing to his new friend
and her father a subsistence, more certain than the will of Helena could afford.
Her death he considered as an event
equally remote and undesirable. This
event, however unexpectedly, had now
happened, and precluded the necessity of
further consideration on this head.

Constantia could not but accept this
bequest. Had it been her wish to de-
cline it, it was not in her power, but she

justly regarded the leisure and independence thus conferred upon her, as inestimable benefits. It was a source of unbounded satisfaction on her father's account, who was once more seated in the bosom of affluence. Perhaps in a rational estimate, one of the most fortunate events that could have befallen those persons, was that period of adversity through which they had been doomed to pass. Most of the defects that adhered to the character of Mr. Dudley, had, by this means, been exterminated. He was now cured of those prejudices which his early prosperity had instilled, and which had flowed from luxurious indulgencies. He had learned to estimate himself at his true value, and to sympathize with sufferings which he himself had partaken.

It was easy to perceive in what light Constantia was regarded by her father. He never reflected on his relation to her without rapture. Her qualities were the objects of his adoration. He resigned himself with pleasure to her guidance. The chain of subordination and duties was reversed. By the ascendancy of her genius and wisdom the province of protection and the tribute of homage had devolved upon her. This had resulted from incessant experience of the wisdom of her measures, and the spectacle of her fortitude and skill in every emergency.

It seemed as if but one evil adhered to the condition of this man. His blindness was an impediment to knowledge and enjoyment, of which, the utmost to be hoped was, that he should regard it without pungent regret, and that he should sometimes forget it: that his mind should occasionally stray into foreign paths, and lose itself in sprightly conversations, or benign reveries. This evil, however, was by no means remediless.

A surgeon of uncommon skill had lately arrived from Europe. He was one of the numerous agents and dependants of Ormond, and had been engaged to abdicate his native country for purposes widely remote from his profession. The first use that was made of him was to introduce him to Mr. Dudley. The diseased organs were critically examined, and the patient was, with considerable difficulty, prevailed upon to undergo the necessary operation. His success corresponded with Constantia's wishes, and her father was once more restored to the enjoyment of light.

These were auspicious events—Constantia held herself amply repaid by them for all that she had suffered. These sufferings had indeed been light, when compared with the effects usually experienced by others in a similar condition. Her wisdom had extracted its sting from adversity, and without allowing herself

to feel much of the evils of its reign, had
employed it as an instrument by which
the sum of her present happiness was
increased. Few suffered less in the midst
of poverty than she. No one ever extracted more felicity from the prosperous
reverse.

CHAP. VIII.

When time had somewhat mitigated
the memory of the late disaster, the intercourse between Ormond and Constance
was renewed. The lady did not overlook her obligations to her friend: it was
to him that she was indebted for her father's restoration to sight, and to whom
both owed, essentially, though indirectly,
their present affluence. In her mind gratitude was no perverse or ignoble principle. She viewed this man as the author of extensive benefits, of which her
situation enabled her to judge with more
accuracy than others. It created no bias
on her judgment, or, at least, none of
which she was sensible. Her equity was
perfectly unfettered, and she decided in
a way contrary to his inclination, with as
little scruple as if the benefits had been

I 3

received, not by herself, but by him. She,
indeed, intended his benefit, though she
thwarted his inclinations.

She had few visitants beside himself.
Their interviews were daily and unformal.
The fate of Helena never produced any
reproaches on her part. She saw the
uselessness of recrimination, not only because she desired to produce emotions
different from those which invective is
adapted to excite, but because it was more
just to soothe than to exasperate the inquietudes which haunted him.

She now enjoyed leisure. She had always been solicitous for mental improve-
ment. Any means subservient to this end
were valuable. The conversation of
Ormond was an inexhaustible fund. By
the variety of topics and the excitements
to reflection it supplied, a more plenteous
influx of knowledge was produced than
could have flowed from any other source.
There was no end to the detailing of facts,
and the canvassing of theories:

I have already said that Ormond was engaged in schemes of an arduous and elevated nature. These were the topics of epistolary discussion between him and a certain number of coadjutors, in different parts of the world. In general discourse, it was proper to maintain a uniform silence respecting these, not only because they involved principles and views remote from vulgar apprehension, but because their success, in some measure, depended on their secrecy. He could not give a stronger proof of his confidence in the sagacity and steadiness of Constance than he now gave, by imparting to her his schemes, and requesting her advice and assistance in the progress of them.

His disclosures, however, were imperfect. What knowledge was imparted, instead of appeasing, only tended to inflame her curiosity. His answers to her inquiries were prompt, and at first sight sufficiently explicit, but upon reconsideration, an obscurity seemed to gather round them, to be dispelled by new inter-rogatories. These, in like manner, effected a momentary purpose, but were sure speedily to lead into new conjectures, and re-immerse her in doubts. The task was always new, was always on the point of being finished, and always to be re-commenced.

Ormond aspired to nothing more ardently than to hold the reins of opinion—to exercise absolute power over the conduct of others, not by constraining their limbs, or by exacting obedience to his authority, but in a way of which his subjects should be scarcely conscious. He desired that his guidance should controul their steps, but that his agency, when most effectual, should be least suspected.

If he were solicitous to govern the thoughts of Constantia; or to regulate her condition, the mode which he pursued had hitherto been admirably conducive

to that end. To have found her friend-
less and indigent, accorded, with the most
fortunate exactness, with his views.—
That she should have descended to this
depth, from a prosperous height, and
therefore be a stranger to the torpor
which attends hereditary poverty, and be
qualified rightly to estimate and use the
competence to which, by this means, she
was now restored, was all that his provi-
dence would have prescribed.

Her thoughts were equally obsequious
to his direction. The novelty and gran-
deur of his schemes could not fail to
transport a mind ardent and capacious as
that of Constance. Here his fortune had
been no less propitious. He did not fail
to discover, and was not slow to seize the
advantages flowing thence. By explaining his plans, opportunity was furnished
to lead and to confine her meditations to
the desirable tract. By adding fictitious
embellishments, he adapted it with more
exactness to his purpose. By piece-meal

and imperfect disclosures, her curiosity
was kept alive.

I have described Ormond as having
contracted a passion for Constance. This
passion certainly existed in his heart, but
it must not be conceived to be immu-
table, or to operate independently of all
those impulses and habits which time
had interwoven in his character. The
person and affections of this woman were
the objects sought by him, and which it
was the dearest purpose of his existence
to gain. This was his supreme good,
though the motives to which it was indebted for its pre-eminence in his imagination were numerous and complex.

I have enumerated his opinions on the
subject of wedlock. The question will
obviously occur, whether Constantia was
sought by him with upright or flagitious views. His sentiments and resolutions on this head had for a time fluctu-
ated, but were now stedfast. Marriage
was, in his eyes, hateful and absurd as

ever. Constance was to be obtained by
any means. If other terms were rejected, he was willing, for the sake of
this good, to accept her as a wife; but
this was a choice to be made only when
every expedient was exhausted, for re-
conciling her to a compact of a different
kind.

For this end he prescribed to himself
a path suited to the character of this
lady. He made no secret of his sentiments and views. He avowed his love,
and described without scruple the scope
of his wishes. He challenged her to
confute his principles, and promised a
candid audience and profound consideration to her arguments. Her present
opinions he knew to be adverse to his
own, but he hoped to change them by
subtilty and perseverance. His further
hopes and designs he concealed from her.
She was unaware, that if he were unable
to effect a change in her creed, he was
determined to adopt a system of impos-

ture—to assume the guise of a convert
to her doctrines, and appear as devout as
herself in his notions of the sanctity of
marriage.

Perhaps it was not difficult to have
foreseen the consequence of these pro-
jects. Constantia's peril was imminent.
This arose not only from the talents and
address of Ormond, but from the community of sentiment which already existed between them. She was unguarded
in a point, where, if not her whole, yet,
doubtless, her principal security and
strongest bulwark would have existed.
She was unacquainted with religion.—
She was unhabituated to conform herself
to any standard, but that connected with
the present life. Matrimonial, as well
as every other human duty, was disconnected in her mind with any awful or
divine sanction. She formed her estimate
of good and evil on nothing but terres-
trial and visible consequences.

This defect in her character she owed

to her father's system of education. Mr.
Dudley was an adherent to what he conceived to be true religion. No man was
more passionate in his eulogy of his own
form of devotion and belief, or in his
invectives against Atheistical dogmas;
but he reflected that religion assumed
many forms, one only of which is salu-
tary or true, and that truth in this respect
is incompatible with infantile and prema-
ture instruction.

To this subject it was requisite to
apply the force of a mature and unfettered understanding. For this end he
laboured to lead away the juvenile reflections of Constantia from religious
topics, to detain them in the paths of
history and eloquence. To accustom
her to the accuracy of geometrical de-
duction, and to the view of those evils
that have flowed in all ages, from mistaken piety.

In consequence of this scheme her habits rather than her opinions, were unde-

vout. Religion was regarded by her not
with disbelief, but with absolute indifference. Her good sense forbad her to
decide before inquiry, but her modes of
study and reflection were foreign to, and
unfitted her for this species of discussion. Her mind was seldom called to
meditate on this subject, and when it
occurred, her perceptions were vague and
obscure. No objects, in the sphere which
she occupied, were calculated to suggest
to her the importance of investigation
and certainty.

It becomes me to confess, however re-
luctantly, thus much concerning my
friend. However abundantly endowed
in other respects, she was a stranger to
the felicity and excellence flowing from
religion. In her struggles with misfortune, she was supported and cheered by
the sense of no approbation but her own.
A defect of this nature will perhaps be
regarded as of less moment when her
extreme youth is remembered. All opi-

nions in her mind were mutable, inasmuch as the progress of her understanding was incessant.

It was otherwise with Ormond. His disbelief was at once unchangeable and strenuous. The universe was to him a series of events, connected by an undesigning and inscrutable necessity, and an assemblage of forms, to which no beginning or end can be conceived. Instead of transient views and vague ideas, his meditations, on religious points, had been intense. Enthusiasm was added to disbelief, and he not only dissented but abhorred.

He deemed it prudent, however, to disguise sentiments which, if unfolded in their full force, would wear to her the appearance of insanity: but he saw and was eager to improve the advantage which his anti-nuptial creed derived from the unsettled state of her opinions. He was not unaware, likewise, of the auspicious and indispensible co-operation of love.

If this advocate were wanting in her bosom, all his efforts would be in vain. If this pleader were engaged in his behalf, he entertained no doubts of his ultimate success. He conceived that her present situation, all whose comforts were the fruits of his beneficence, and which afforded her no other subject of contemplation than himself, was as favourable as possible to the growth of this passion.

Constance was acquainted with his wishes. She could not fail to see that she might speedily be called upon to determine a momentous question. Her own sensations, and the character of Ormond, were, therefore, scrutinized with suspicious attention. Marriage could be justified in her eyes, only by community of affections and opinions. She might love without the sanction of her judgment; but while destitute of that sanction, she would never suffer it to sway her conduct.

Ormond was imperfectly known. What

knowledge she had gained flowed chiefly
from his own lips, and was therefore unattended with certainty. What portion
of deceit or disguise was mixed with his
conversation could be known only by
witnessing his actions with her own eyes,
and comparing his testimony with that of
others. He had embraced a multitude of
opinions which appeared to her erroneous.
Till these were rectified, and their conclusions were made to correspond, wedlock was improper. Some of these ob-
scurities might be dispelled, and some of
these discords be resolved into harmony
by time. Meanwhile it was proper to
guard the avenues to her heart, and
screen herself from self-delusion.

There was no motive to conceal her
reflections on this topic from her father.
Mr. Dudley discovered, without her assistance, the views of Ormond. His
daughter's happiness was blended with
his own. He lived but in the consciousness of her tranquillity. Her image was

seldom absent from his eyes, and never
from his thoughts. The emotions which
it excited sprung but in part from the
relationship of father. It was gratitude
and veneration which she claimed from
him, and which filled him with rapture.

He ruminated deeply on the character
of Ormond. The political and anti-
theological tenets of this man were regarded, not merely with disapprobation,
but antipathy. He was not ungrateful
for the benefits which had been conferred
upon him. Ormond's peculiarities of
sentiment excited no impatience, as long
as he was regarded merely as a visitant.
It was only as one claiming to possess his
daughter, that his presence excited in
Mr. Dudley trepidation and loathing.

Ormond was unacquainted with what
was passing in the mind of Mr. Dudley.
The latter conceived his own benefactor
and his daughter's friend to be entitled
to the most scrupulous and affable ur-
banity. His objections to a nearer al-

liance were urged with frequent and pathetic vehemence only in his private interviews with Constance. Ormond and
he seldom met. Mr. Dudley, as soon as
his sight was perfectly retrieved, betook
himself with eagerness to painting, an
amusement which his late privations had
only contributed to endear to him.

Things remained nearly on their present footing for some months. At the
end of this period some engagement
obliged Ormond to leave the city. He
promised to return with as much speed
as circumstances would admit. Meanwhile his letters supplied her with topics
of reflection. These were frequently received, and were models of that energy
of style which results from simplicity of
structure, from picturesque epithets, and
from the compression of much meaning
into few words. His arguments seldom
imparted conviction; but delight never
failed to flow from their lucid order and

cogent brevity. His narratives were un-
equalled for rapidity and comprehensive-
ness. Every sentence was a treasury to
moralists and painters.

CHAP. IX.

DOMESTIC and studious occupations
did not wholly engross the attention of
Constance. Social pleasures were precious to her heart, and she was not backward to form fellowships and friendships
with those around her. Hitherto she had
met with no one entitled to an uncommon
portion of regard, or worthy to supply
the place of the friend of her infancy.
Her visits were rare, and as yet chiefly
confined to the family of Mr. Melbourne.
Here she was treated with flattering distinctions, and enjoyed opportunities of
extending as far as she pleased her con-
nections with the gay and opulent. To
this she felt herself by no means inclined,
and her life was still eminently distinguished by love of privacy and habits of
seclusion.

One morning, feeling an indisposition to abstraction, she determined to drop in for an hour on Mrs. Melbourne. Finding Mrs. Melbourne's parlour unoccupied, she proceeded unceremoniously to an apartment on the second floor, where that lady was accustomed to sit. She entered, but this room was likewise empty. Here she cast her eyes on a, collection of prints, copied from the Farnese collection, and employed herself for some minutes in comparing the forms of Titiano and the Caracchi.

Suddenly notes of peculiar sweetness were wafted to her ear from without. She listened with surprise, for the tones of her father's lute were distinctly recognized. She went to the window, which chanced to look into a back court. The music was perceived to come from the window of the next house. She recollected her interview with the purchaser of her instrument at the music shop, and the powerful impression which the stranger's countenance had made upon her.

The first use she had made of her recent change of fortune was to endeavour to recover this instrument. The music dealer, when reminded of the purchase, and interrogated as to the practicability of regaining the lute, for which she was willing to give treble the price, answered that he had no knowledge of the foreign lady, beyond what was gained at the interview which took place in Constantia's presence. Of her name, residence, and condition, he knew nothing, and had endeavoured in vain to acquire knowledge.

Now this incident seemed to have furnished her with the information she had so earnestly sought. This performer was probably the stranger herself. Her residence so near the Melbournes, and in a house which was the property of the magistrate, might be means of information as to her condition, and perhaps of introduction to a personal acquaintance.

While engaged in these reflections Mrs. Melbourne entered the apartment. Constantia related this incident to her friend, and stated the motives of her present curiosity. Her friend willingly imparted what knowledge she possessed relative to this subject. This was the sum—

This house had been hired previously to the appearance of the yellow fever by an English family, who left their native soil with a view to a permanent abode in the new world. They had scarcely taken possession of the dwelling when they were terrified by the progress of the epidemic. They had fled from the danger; but this circumstance, in addition to some others, induced them to change their scheme. An evil so unwonted as pestilence impressed them with a belief of perpetual danger as long as they remained on this side of the ocean. They prepared for an immediate return to England.

For this end their house was relinquished, and their splendid furniture destined to be sold by auction. Before this event could take place, application was made to Mr. Melbourne by a lady, whom his wife's description shewed to be the same person of whom Constantia was in search. She not only rented the house, but negociated by means of her landlord for the purchase of the furniture.

Her servants were blacks, and all but one, who officiated as steward, unacquainted with the English language. Some accident had proved her name to be Beauvais. She had no visitants; very rarely walked abroad, and then only in the evening with a female servant in attendance. Her hours appeared to be divided between the lute and the pen. As to her previous history, or her present sources of subsistence, Mrs. Melbourne's curiosity had not been idle, but no consistent information was obtainable. Some incidents had given birth to the conjecture that she was wife, or daughter, or sister of Beauvais, the partizan of Brissot, whom the faction of Marat had lately consigned to the scaffold; but this conjecture was unsupported by suitable evidence.

This tale by no means diminished Constantia's desire of personal intercourse. She saw no means of effecting her purpose. Mrs. Melbourne was unqualified to introduce her, having been discouraged in all the advances she had made towards a more friendly intercourse. Constance reflected, that her motives to seclusion would probably induce this lady to treat others as her friend had been treated.

It was possible, however, to gain access to her, if not as a friend, yet as the original proprietor of the lute. She determined to employ the agency of Roseveldt, the music seller, for the pur-

pose of re-buying this instrument. To
enforce her application, she commissioned
this person, whose obliging temper entitled him to confidence, to state her in-
ducements for originally offering it for
sale, and her motives for desiring the re-
possession on any terms which the lady
thought proper to dictate.

Roseveldt fixed an hour in which it
was convenient for him to execute her
commission. This hour having passed,
Constance, who was anxious respecting
his success, hastened to his house. Roseveldt delivered the instrument, which the
lady, having listened to his pleas and
offers, directed to be gratuitously restored to Constance. At first she had
expressed her resolution to part with it
on no account, and at no price. Its
music was her only recreation, and this
instrument surpassed any she had ever
before seen in the costliness and delicacy
of its workmanship. But Roseveldt's re-

presentations produced an instant change
of resolution, and she not only eagerly
consented to restore it, but refused to receive any thing in payment.

Constantia was deeply affected by this
unexpected generosity. It was not her
custom to be outstripped in this career.
She now condemned herself for her eagerness so regain this instrument. During
her father's blindness it was a powerful,
because the only solace of his melancholy. Now he had no longer the same
anxieties to encounter, and books and
the pencil were means of gratification
always at hand. The lute, therefore, she
imagined could be easily dispensed with
by Mr. Dudley, whereas its power of
consoling might be as useful to the unknown lady as it had formerly been to
her father. She readily perceived in what
manner it became her to act. Roseveldt
was commissioned to re-deliver the lute,
and to entreat the lady's acceptance of it.

The tender was received without hesitation, and Roseveldt dismissed without any inquiry relative to Constance.

These transactions were reflected on by Constance with considerable earnestness. The conduct of the stranger, her affluent and lonely state, her conjectural relationship to the actors in the great theatre of Europe, were mingled together in the fancy of Constance, and embellished with the conceptions of her beauty derived from their casual meeting at Roseveldt's. She forgot not their similitude in age and sex, and delighted to prolong the dream of future confidence and friendship to take place between them. Her heart sighed for a companion fitted to partake in all her sympathies.

This strain, by being connected with the image of a being like herself, who had grown up with her from childhood, who had been entwined with her earliest affections, but from whom she had been severed from the period at which her

father's misfortunes commenced, and of
whose present condition she was wholly
ignorant, was productive of the deepest
melancholy. It filled her with excru-
ciating, and for a time irremediable sad-
ness. It formed a kind of paroxysm,
which like some febrile affections, approach and retire without warning, and
against the most vehement struggles.

In this mood her fancy was thronged
with recollections of scenes in which her
friend had sustained a part. Their last
interview was commonly revived in her
remembrance so forcibly, as almost to
produce a lunatic conception of its reality. A ditty which they sung together on
that occasion flowed to her lips. If ever
human tones were qualified to convey the
whole soul, they were those of Constance
when she sung—

> The breeze awakes, the bark prepares,
>   To waft me to a distant shore :
> But far beyond this world of cares
>   We meet again to part no more.

These fits were accustomed to approach and to vanish by degrees. They were transitory but not unfrequent, and were pregnant with such agonizing tenderness, such heart-breaking sighs, and a flow of such bitter yet delicious tears, that it were not easily decided whether the pleasure or the pain surmounted. When symptoms of their coming were felt she hastened into solitude, that the progress of her feelings might endure no restraint.

On the evening of the day on which the lute had been sent to the foreign lady, Constantia was alone in her chamber immersed in desponding thoughts. From these she was recalled by Fabian her black servant, who announced a guest. She was loath to break off the thread of her present meditations, and inquired with a tone of some impatience who the guest was. The servant was unable to tell; it was a young lady whom he

K 4

had never before seen. She had opened the door herself, and entered the parlour without previous notice.

Constance paused at this relation. Her thoughts had recently been fixed upon Sophia Westwyn. Since their parting four years before she had heard no tidings of this woman. Her fears imagined no more probable cause of her friend's silence than her death. This, however, was uncertain. The question now occurred, and brought with it sensations that left her no power to move: was this the guest?

Her doubts were quickly dispelled, for the stranger taking a light from the table, and not brooking the servant's delays, followed Fabian to the chamber of his mistress. She entered with careless freedom,. and presented to the astonished eyes of Constantia the figure she had met at Roseveldt's, and the purchaser of her lute.

The stranger advanced towards her with quick steps, and mingling tones of benignity and sprightliness, said :

I have come to perform a duty. I have received from you to-day a lute that I valued almost as my best friend. To find another in America, would not, perhaps, be possible ; but certainly none equally superb and exquisite as this can be found. To shew how highly I esteem the gift, I come in person to thank you for it.—Here she stopped.

Constance could not suddenly recover from the extreme surprise into which the unexpectedness of this meeting had thrown her. She could scarcely sufficiently suppress this confusion to enable her to reply to these rapid effusions of her visitant, who resumed, with augmented freedom :

I came, as I said, to thank you, but to say the truth that was not all. I came likewise to see you. Having done my errand, I suppose I must go. I would

K 5

fain stay longer and talk to you a little.
Will you give me leave?

Constance, scarcely retrieving her
composure, stammered out a polite assent. They seated themselves, and the
visitant, pressing the hand she had taken,
proceeded in a strain so smooth, so flowing, sliding from grave to gay, blending
vivacity with tenderness, interpreting
Constantia's silence with such keen sagacity, and accounting for the singularities
of her own deportment in a way so respectful to her companion, and so worthy of a stedfast and pure mind in herself, that every embarrassment and scruple were quickly banished from their
interview.

In an hour the guest took her leave.
No promise of repeating her visit, and
no request that Constantia would repay
it, was made. Their parting seemed to
be the last; whatever purpose having
been contemplated, appeared to be accomplished by this transient meeting. It

was of a nature deeply to interest the mind of Constance. This was the lady who talked with Roseveldt, and bargained with Melbourne, and they had been induced by appearances to suppose her ignorant of any language but French; but her discourse on the present occasion was in English, and was distinguished by unrivalled fluency. Her phrases and habits of pronouncing were untinctured by any foreign mixture, and bespoke the perfect knowledge of a native of America.

On the next evening, while Constantia was reviewing this transaction, calling up and weighing the sentiments which the stranger had uttered, and indulging some regret at the unlikelihood of their again meeting, Martinette (for I will henceforth call her by her true name) entered the apartment as abruptly as before. She accounted for the visit merely by the pleasure it afforded her, and proceeded in a strain even more versatile and brilliant than before. This interview ended like the first, without any tokens on the part of the guest of resolution or desire to renew it, but a third interview took place on the ensuing day.

Henceforth Martinette became a frequent but hasty visitant, and Constantia became daily more enamoured of her new acquaintance. She did not overlook peculiarities in the conversation and deportment of this woman. These exhibited no tendencies to confidence or traces of sympathy. They merely denoted large experience, vigorous faculties, and masculine attainments. Herself was never introduced, except as an observer, but her observations on government and manners were profound and critical.

Her education seemed not widely different from that which Constantia had received. It was classical and mathematical, but to this was added a knowledge of political and military transactions in Europe during the present age, which implied the possession of better means of information than books. She depicted scenes and characters with the accuracy of one who had partaken and witnessed them herself.

Constantia's attention had been chiefly occupied by personal concerns. Her youth had passed in contention with misfortune, or in the quietudes of study. She could not be unapprized of cotemporary revolutions and wars, but her ideas concerning them were indefinite and vague. Her views and her inferences on this head were general and speculative. Her acquaintance with history was exact and circumstantial, in proportion as she retired backward from her own age. She knew more of the siege of Mutina than that of Lisle; more of the machinations of Cataline and the tumults of Clodius, than of the prostration of the Bastile, and the proscriptions of Marat.

She listened, therefore, with unspeakable eagerness to this reciter, who detailed to her, as the occasion suggested, the progress of action and opinion on the theatre of France and Poland. Conceived and rehearsed as this was with the energy and copiousness of one who sustained a part in the scene, the mind of Constantia was always kept at the pitch of curiosity and wonder.

But while this historian described the features, personal deportment, and domestic character of Antonette, Mirabeau and Robespierre, an impenetrable veil was drawn over her own condition. There was a warmth and freedom in her details which bespoke her own co-agency in these events, but was unattended by transports of indignation or sorrow, or by pauses of abstraction, such as were likely to occur in one whose hopes and fears had been intimately blended with public events.

Constance could not but derive humi-

liation from comparing her own slender
acquirements with those of her companion. She was sensible that all the dif-
ferences between them arose from diver-
sities of situation. She was eager to
discover in what particulars this diversity
consisted. She was for a time withheld
by scruples, not easily explained, from
disclosing her wishes. An accident,
however, occurred to remove these im-
pediments. One evening this uncere-
monious visitant dicovered Constance
busily surveying a chart of the Mediter-
ranean Sea. This circumstance led the
discourse to the present state of Syria
and Cyprus. Martinette was copious in
her details. Constance listened for a
time, and when a pause ensued, questioned her companion as to the means she
possessed of acquiring so much knowledge. This question was proposed
with diffidence, and prefaced by apo-
logies.

Instead of being offended by your question, replied the guest, I only wonder that it never before occurred to you. Travellers tell us much. Volney and Mariti would have told you nearly all that I have told. With these I have conversed personally, as well as read their books, but my knowledge is in truth a species of patrimony. I inherit it.

Will you be good enough, said Constance, to explain yourself?

My mother was a Greek of Cyprus. My father was a Sclavonian of Ragusa, and I was born in a garden at Aleppo.

That was a singular concurrence.

How singular? That a nautical vagrant like my father should sometimes anchor in the bay of Naples; that a Cyprian merchant should carry his property and daughter beyond the reach of a Turkish Sangiack, and seek an asylum so commodious as Napoli; that my father should have dealings with this merchant, see, love, and marry his daughter, and afterwards procure from the French government a consular commission to Aleppo; that the union should in due time be productive of a son and daughter, are events far from being singular. They happen daily.

And may I venture to ask if this be your history?

The history of my parents. I hope you do not consider the place of my birth as the sole or the most important circumstance of my life.

: Nothing would please me more than to be enabled to compare it with other incidents. I am apt to think that your life is a tissue of surprising events. That the daughter of a Ragusan and Greek should have seen and known so much; that she should talk English with equal fluency and more correctness than a native; that I should now be conversing with her in a corner so remote from

Cyprus and Sicily, are events more wonderful than any which I have known.

Wonderful! Pish! Thy ignorance, thy miscalculation of probabilities is far more so. My father talked to me in Sclavonic; my mother and her maids talked to me in Greek. My neighbours talked to me in a medley of Arabic, Syriac, and Turkish. My father's secretary was a scholar. He was as well versed in Lysias and Xenophon as any of their cotemporaries. He laboured for ten years to enable me to read a language essentially the same with that I used daily to my nurse and mother. Is it wonderful then that I should be skilful in Sclavonic, Greek, and the jargon of Aleppo? To have refrained from learning was impossible. Suppose a girl, prompt, diligent, inquisitive, to spend ten years of her life partly in Spain, partly in Tuscany, partly in France, and partly in England. With her versatile curiosity

and flexible organs would it be possible
for her to remain ignorant of each of
these languages? Latin is the mother of
them all, and presents itself of course to
her studious attention.

I cannot easily conceive motives which
should lead you before the age of twen-
ty through so many scenes.

Can you not? You grew and flourish-
ed, like a frail Mimosa, in the spot
where destiny had planted you. Thank
my stars, I am somewhat better than a
vegetable. Necessity, it is true, and not
choice, set me in motion, but I am not
sorry for the consequences.

Is it too much, said Constance, with
some hesitation, to request a detail of
your youthful adventures?

Too much to give, perhaps, at a short
notice. To such as you my tale might
abound with novelty, while to others,
more acquainted with vicissitudes, it
would be tedious and flat. I must be

gone in a few minutes. For that and for better reasons, I must not be minute. A summary at present will enable you to judge how far a more copious narrative is suited to instruct or to please you.

END OF VOL. II.

B. Clarke, Printer, Well-Street, London.